C000137124

For Imogen who encouraged the writing
of this book and my step-grandchildren,
Nick, Holly, and Lucy

First published in Great Britain, October 2015

Text copyright © Susan Williamson

Illustration copyright © Carrie Hill

Photograph page 9 © Historic England

SerenArts Publishing
Unit 3, Tithebarn Workshops
Pound Lane, Bradford-on-Avon
Wiltshire BA15 1LF

Designer: Sally Geeve

Editor/indexer: Rosemary Cole

The text of this book is set in ITC Garamond

ISBN
978 0 9932949 0 7

Printed and bound in Great Britain by
JFDi Print Services

www.theallotmentkitchen.com

THE ALLOTMENT  KITCHEN

FAVOURITE RECIPES AND IDEAS

A COLLECTION
BY SUSAN WILLIAMSON

ILLUSTRATIONS BY
CARRIE HILL

DESIGN BY
SALLY GEEVE

CONTENTS

Apples 11

Artichokes, Globe 19

Artichokes, Jerulsalem 23

Asparagus 25

Beans, broad 33

Beans, runner, French, Blue Lake 37

Beetroot 41

Broccoli 47

Brussels sprouts 51

Cabbage 53

Carrots 57

Cauliflower 61

Cavalo Nero and kale 65

Celery and celeriac 69

Chicory, endive, radicchio and Treviso 73

Courgettes and marrow 77

Cucumber 83

Currants, black, red and white 87

Fennel 93

Garlic 97

Gooseberries 99

Hedgerow 103

CONTENTS

Herbs and weeds   113

Leeks   123

Lettuce   129

Onions and shallots   134

Parsnips   140

Pears   145

Peas   151

Plums and greengages   156

Potatoes   161

Pumpkins and squashes   167

Raspberries   171

Rhubarb   179

Spinach   185

Strawberries   189

Swedes   194

Sweetcorn   196

Swiss chard   199

Tomatoes   201

Turnips   207

Pastries, sauces and desserts   209

Acknowledgements and bibliography   222

Index   225

INTRODUCTION

This book contains favourite recipes and ideas collected over twenty five years of having an allotment. Produce from the allotment becomes a key ingredient, the start of planning a meal. Writing has been a perpetual diary, recording those recipes which have given great pleasure. Without an allotment or vegetable patch it would be difficult to imagine the thrill of marking the year with seasonal pleasures. The first rhubarb, tender asparagus shoots, sweetcorn freshly picked, young broad beans to be eaten whole, the start of the strawberry season, and the first new potatoes freshly dug are all cause for celebration. It is a delightful bonus when home grown vegetables give pleasure as part of a meal.

The recipes might have stayed as my own private notebook but for my daughter's suggestion that I should publish them. It was neighbour Carrie Hill's perfectly illustrated 'thank you' note for a bunch of our asparagus that made me realise that I had found an illustrator. The book was propelled from idea to completion after Carrie introduced me to Sally Geeve, who has designed the book with a brilliant eye for detail. My good friend Rosemary Cole has been kind enough to read each chapter and prepare the index. I am very grateful to them all. It has been a happy coincidence to have so much talent close at hand.

Our allotment is behind the garden wall. Living in Bath, only a short walk from the city centre, the allotment site seems a place of escape, the country within the city. Foxes, badgers, rats, ducks, rabbits, and even deer, make regular visits. I try, in a desultory way, to garden organically. The wood pigeons take every opportunity to ruin our crops and the mice are suspected of mischief. Slugs and snails do their damage; some years are marked by blight or pests. In any year crops can fail but others flourish. Allotment holders soon learn to cope with mixed fortunes.

Marlborough Buildings, where we live, is to the west of the Royal Crescent, and it is commonly held to have been built as a windbreak for John Wood's design. The land behind was, and is today, mostly parkland. By the middle of World War II, with fresh food becoming increasingly scarce, allotments had been established in front of the Royal Crescent and beyond to Royal Victoria Park and the golf course.

This photo, dated 1945, shows how desolate the site was at that time with no trees or bushes and only a few Brussels sprouts and possibly potatoes. Allotments were calculated to be large enough to keep a family of four in vegetables for a year. The necessity of survival in wartime Britain did not allow for fun.

In the years since WWII the allotment movement has changed. The introduction of a hobby element is undeniable but something of the old spirit survives. On summer evenings we may be queuing at the trough and jokingly talk of installing a sprinkler system. We share seeds or arrange communal bonfires. The landscape has changed. Now there are bushes and fruit cages. Compost bins dot the landscape.

I write in mid-November. The cats hear the key in the back door turn and scamper out with me. After squally rain, it is calm but cold with piercing blue sky. The leaves are sodden on the ground. Overnight frost has caught the nasturtiums and lovage but signs of spring are already present; the overwintering onions show green shoots and next year's fennel is evident. It is time to plant the broad beans, the soil is prepared, but today there are leeks to be picked, the first of the autumn, and the last Wellington apples to gather. I greet an allotment neighbour as I walk over to my husband's plot. His chard gives some good ideas for tomorrow's supper.

Onions, asparagus, rhubarb, broad beans, raspberries and salads are among our staple crops. We have two onion beds that we use for the main crops of red and golden globe onions, and the Japanese onion sets, sown in October. Space is also found in these beds for the leeks transplanted in August. Chinese leaves self-seed effortlessly and are weeded more than picked for use in a salad or stir-fry. Asparagus is fed healthy heaps of manure. Gooseberries need little attention and rhubarb must be the easiest crop of all, needing only generous helpings of well-rotted manure spread over twice a year. With careful gleaning, ingredients for a salad can usually be found throughout the year.

Herbs are vital to my cooking. Bay leaves, sage and rosemary can always be picked. Mint, lovage, sweet Cicely and tansy return each year like old friends. The meals we anticipate the most are the ones that can only happen in years of an especially good harvest or when certain fruits coincide; elderflowers and gooseberries that can be made into a fool, peaches and raspberries turned into a parfait, rhubarb and sweet Cicely in a crumble, or broad beans and artichokes in a vegetable stew.

I have included a hedgerow element in this book. Brambling late in summer is one of my favourite pastimes. Brambles, hawthorns, crab apples, medlars and walnuts thrive on the edge of the allotment site. Wild garlic is found in many shady spots during May and horseradish here in Somerset can be found by the roadside. Damsons, wild apples, and sloes are found beside the footpaths around the city. Bath asparagus, Star of Bethlehem, is now protected but was once harvested daily to supply the food markets of London.

We freeze little and eat our way through the season. Of course, it is useful to have supplies of fruit purée, blanched peas and beans in the deep freeze for the lean early months of the year but nothing surpasses the delight in having freshly picked produce. Jams, chutneys and pickles are, however, a valued part of our store.

A word on measurements; for cakes and puddings the measurements are precise but, for the rest, I give a guide. Use what is available; you will know how many you are cooking for. Make more or less depending what you have harvested. I hope this book will encourage cooks to experiment. If you are lacking one spice used in a recipe, it will not matter but be wary of adding what is not required.

Inspiration for this book has come from many sources. The recipe writers I most admire include Elizabeth David, Anna del Conte, Mark Hix's articles in the Saturday edition of *The Independent*, Simon Hopkinson, Yotam Ottolenghi, Hugh Fearnley-Whittingstall and Nigel Slater. More ideas have come, over the years, from friends and family.

I hope you will enjoy these recipes and that they provide you not only with good meals but ideas for many more.

APPLES

A pples and cheese, preferably good Cheddar cheese, are such a perfect combination. The taste conjures up an image of haymaking and autumn idyll. With the expansion of farmers' markets and farm shops, it is good to see so many old varieties of apple becoming available again.

As I write this we are picking up buckets of windfalls daily. Already the racks in the vaults are full of the apples that we hope will last us through the winter and the rest must be processed, given away and enjoyed. We have been careful with our choice of apple trees. Cox's Orange Pippin and Bramley's Seedling were the first planted and are now over 20 years old. Some years they have a heavy prune. Next came Beauty of Bath, one of the best early apples. My aunt is a great tree expert and it was her advice that introduced us to the superbly flavoured Tydeman's Late Orange and Orléans Reinette.

At the top of the allotment we planted more cooking apple trees; Lord Derby, which cooks to a pleasant red, Rev. W Wilks, which the Scotts Nursery catalogue describes as cooking to a 'pale yellow froth'. Our last tree is Wellington. It produces a late acid-flavoured apple that is traditionally used in making mincemeat.

"I will make an end of my dinner; there's pippins and cheese to come."

William Shakespeare,
Merry Wives of Windsor
Act 1, scene 4

APPLE SNOW

My version of apple snow is probably not that at all but, whatever its name, it is certainly a family favourite. A purée of sweetened, cooked apples allowed to cool with about a third of its volume of whipped double cream gently stirred in. A stiffly whisked egg white can be folded in to give lightness.

BAKED APPLES

A simple dessert with endless possibilities but the quality and shape of the apple is crucial. Bramley's that are not too big work well, and it is worth trying other varieties such as Monarch.

Wash and core the apples and mark a line round their widest circumference. Fill the centres with sultanas and sugar. Ground almonds and dates are also good fillers and you may add a knob of butter, or brandy butter, on the top of each fruit. Stand in a shallow

dish into which a little water and some sugar has been added. Cook at 180°C for about 45 minutes but check regularly towards the end of cooking to be sure the skins are not blackening or the fruit exploding.

Serve warm with cream or custard.

HOT APPLE AND CALVADOS SOUFFLÉ

2 tbsp melted butter

55g caster sugar, plus extra for
   dusting soufflé dish or ramekins

150g Bramley apple purée

1 tbsp Calvados

2 tsp corn flour

2 medium egg whites

Brush the soufflé dish with melted butter and sprinkle with a little of the caster sugar.

Stir the Calvados into the corn flour, then mix together with the apple purée and half the remaining sugar. Cook gently in a heavy bottomed pan for 1-2 minutes, stirring constantly with a wooden spoon until the mixture has thickened. Transfer to a bowl and cover.

Whisk the egg whites in a clean bowl until they form soft peaks. Add remaining sugar and whisk again until glossy. Whisk a third of the egg white mixture into the apple purée to loosen it and then, using a metal spoon, fold in the remaining egg white. Spoon the mixture into the prepared dish and bake for 7-8 minutes in a hot oven.

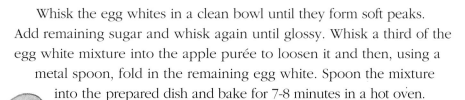

Serve immediately.

Apple and Blackberry Pie

300g puff pastry (bought or home-made)
3 medium sized apples, peeled, cored and
   cut into slices
A punnet or more of blackberries
Sugar to taste

Lightly stew the apples with sugar until they begin to soften, then add the blackberries for the last minutes of cooking. Leave to one side to cool.

Have ready a buttered 20-22cm diameter pie dish. Cut the pastry into two unequal sections. Wrap the smaller in cling film and put in the fridge. On a floured board, roll out the larger to line the pastry dish. Spread the apple mixture over the pie base and, with a pastry brush, moisten the pastry rim with a little of the apple liquid.

Roll out the remaining pastry into a circle and place on top of the pie. Press the edges together to seal the rim. Using a knife, trim excess pastry from the edges.

Brush a little milk over the top of the pie, cut a slash in the centre to allow the steam to escape and cook it in an oven heated to 180°C for about 30 minutes or until the crust is nicely browned. Towards the end of cooking, put the pie on the floor of the oven for five minutes or so to be sure the base is cooked.

Serve hot or cold with cream or custard.

Quinces, cinnamon, cloves or sultanas could flavour the pie in place of the blackberries. The same recipe could be used for plums, greengages, rhubarb, blackcurrants or apricots but take care that the pie filling is not too liquid. Any excess liquid can be made into a sauce to be served with the pie or kept for use in a jelly.

Mincemeat for Christmas

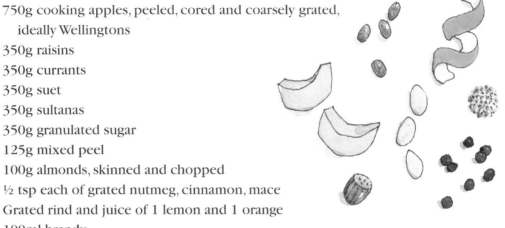

Homemade mincemeat is in a different league to most shop bought ones. It keeps well, and if it does begin to dry out, can always be revived with extra brandy.

750g cooking apples, peeled, cored and coarsely grated,
    ideally Wellingtons
350g raisins
350g currants
350g suet
350g sultanas
350g granulated sugar
125g mixed peel
100g almonds, skinned and chopped
½ tsp each of grated nutmeg, cinnamon, mace
Grated rind and juice of 1 lemon and 1 orange
100ml brandy

Mix the orange and lemon juice with the brandy. Put all the other ingredients into a large bowl, mix well and add the brandy and juices. Pack into kilner jars and store.

Dried Apples

Place cored rings of apples about 1 cm thick from the central part of the apple on a wire rack and dry in the oven at a low temperature for 4 – 18 hours until they have the feel of chamois leather. Leave to cool on kitchen paper then store in kilner jars.

If the apples are not dried out sufficiently, they will quickly become mouldy. If in any doubt, they can be stored in the deep freeze and brought out in small batches. These are very good for putting in school packed lunches and will keep for several months.

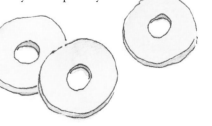

TARTE TATIN

250g puff pastry (bought or home-made)
6–7 dessert apples
250g granulated sugar
100g butter

Using a tatin or flameproof pie dish make a caramel with half the sugar and a spoonful or two of water. Take it off the heat before it becomes too dark. Sprinkle over half the remaining sugar and dot on the butter. A spoonful of brandy could also be added.

Peel, core and cut the apples into segments and lay them in a sunflower pattern on top of the caramel. Sprinkle over the rest of the sugar.

Roll out the pastry and cut a circle the size of the pie dish, place it on top of the apples taking care that all that the edges of the pie are turned in. Fork over it to create some air holes.

Bake at 180°C for about 45 minutes or until the crust is nicely browned. Run a knife around the edge of the pie, invert it onto a plate, and serve either hot or cold.

Pear Tarte Tatin is made in the same way.

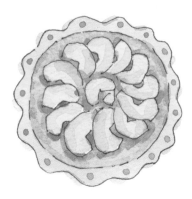

Tarte aux Pommes

It does not seem extravagant to have two French inspired recipes for apple tarts. This one is a show piece, requiring fancy work, and tastes as good as it looks. It is also creative. The shape of the tart and placement of the apples become, by default, a work of art.

225g sablée pastry (see page 214)
500g dessert apples
Caster sugar
Puréed apricot jam

Lightly butter a baking tray. Take the pastry from the fridge and roll it out, working quickly. Sablée pastry is fragile; it sticks easily and it is best to keep it lightly dusted with flour. Turn the pastry a few times while rolling it out to ensure evenness.

Transfer the pastry to the buttered tray and spread it out to form either a circle or a rectangle. If, during this process, the pastry should tear, don't worry as it can easily be patched up. Turn up the edges to form a border.

Core and peel the apples and then cut in half vertically. Cut into thin crosswise slices.

Arrange the slices, overlapping, on the pastry. Sprinkle the surface with sugar and bake at 180°C for 30 minutes and then continue cooking for about 15 minutes with the tart placed on the floor of the oven until it is cooked.

Paint the apple slices with the heated jam purée. Transfer to a plate for serving either warm or cold.

APPLE JELLY

This jelly is delicious on its own account but also forms the basis for herb and spice jellies such as mint, scented geranium or chilli. Apple can also be mixed with other fruits such as brambles and damsons or elderberries. The best apples to use for all these jellies are the small, bitter apples that grow wild but any cooking apples can be used and windfalls are perfect.

Take a good number of apples. Wash them and cut away any bruised or damaged bits and chop the apples into pieces. Put into a preserving pan and almost cover with water. Bring to the boil slowly and then let simmer, stirring occasionally to ensure that no apples are sticking. Cook until the apples are soft. Allow to cool and then drain overnight through muslin.

Measure the juice and transfer to a preserving pan. The old equation of a pound of sugar to a pint of liquid in metric terms becomes five liquid to four sugar. Or put simply, for every 1.25 litre of liquid, 1kg of sugar is needed.

Heat the juice slowly and add the warmed sugar. Allow to boil and then reduce the heat, letting the jelly bubble steadily until it is set.

Pour into warmed clean jars.

ARTICHOKES, GLOBE

Globe artichokes are a cultivated variety of thistle and were well known to the ancient Greeks and Romans. The ones we grow are small, never aspiring to the big, fleshy, purple tinged continental varieties. Artichokes have been cultivated in England since the Middle Ages. In 1530, they were reported as growing in Henry VIII's garden at Newhall.

Pick artichokes young before they become tough and the chokes are formed. Thistles are decorative and any that become too old to cook can be left to flower, not only brightening the allotment but also attracting bees and butterflies.

There are some caveats for cooking globe artichokes. Take care while preparing artichokes as they stain hands and nails. Every recipe repeats the instruction to keep a half lemon or lemon-infused water to hand to prevent the artichokes from discolouring during preparation. In addition, it is important not to use aluminum or iron pots which not only blacken the artichokes but give them an unpleasant taste.

Globe artichokes go especially well with broad beans and lamb. Thyme is the herb which accompanies them best. Raw slivers of prepared artichokes, infused with olive oil and lemon juice, give interest to spring salads.

Raw Artichoke Salad

With a bowl of lemon-infused water to hand in which to place the artichokes as they are being prepared, remove the stalk and take off the tough outer leaves of the artichoke. Once you have reached the softer, pale leaves, cut across the artichoke tips to be left with the bottom third. With a paring knife, remove any residual green bits to leave only the flesh. Cut the artichoke in half and remove the choke or thistle.

With a mandoline or sharp knife, cut the artichoke into thin slivers and immediately put them in a bowl and dress with lemon juice and olive oil. Leave for a while for the dressing to infuse, then season with salt and pepper and add to a mixed salad.

Artichokes, Parboiled and Braised

This is an easy way to use young artichokes which makes an excellent accompaniment to any lamb dish.

Take off a few rounds of the bottom leaves and the tips. Cut the artichokes into quarters and place them in a bowl of water flavoured with lemon juice as they are prepared. Boil gently in salted water for five minutes. Drain and, when cool enough, cut out the choke. Cut the artichoke pieces in half. Place in a roasting dish. Sprinkle over some olive oil and less vinegar or lemon juice. Lay over a few sprigs of thyme. Cook in a roasting oven for about ten minutes.

Artichokes alla Italiana

Take about 12 very young artichokes and cut off the bases and almost half the tops. Pull off about three layers of leaves until only the tender parts remain. Cut the artichokes into quarters and brush them with lemon juice.

Put the artichoke pieces into a heavy bottomed pan and barely cover them with water, half a glass of olive oil, salt, and freshly ground black pepper. Cook gently for about 15 minutes until almost all the liquid has evaporated. Add the juice of half a lemon.

Serve hot or cold, sprinkled with chopped parsley.

Artichokes, Peas and Broad Beans

A summer treat inspired by a Greek recipe.

4 young artichokes
4 tbsp olive oil
1 large onion, thinly sliced
150g shelled fresh peas
150g shelled fresh broad beans
1 tsp capers
Salt and freshly ground black pepper

Prepare the artichokes by removing the stalks, outer leaves and tips. Cut into quarters and remove any chokes. Place the sections in a bowl of lemon-infused water as they are prepared. Heat oil in a saucepan and gently cook the onion until softened. Add the peas, broad beans, artichokes and capers. Add enough water to barely cover. Season. Put the lid on the pan and cook gently for about 20 minutes, stirring occasionally, until the vegetables are tender.

Provençal Artichokes

12 small artichokes
4 cloves garlic, peeled
2 medium sized onions, finely sliced
1 carrot, peeled, cut into very small cubes
1 stem of thyme
1 bay leaf
1 lemon
½ glass white wine
A ladle or two chicken or vegetable bouillon
Salt and freshly ground black pepper

Remove the tougher leaves at the base of the artichokes but leave 2cm of the stalks. With a paring knife, remove all green parts of the artichoke, even on the stalks. Cut the artichokes in half and place them in a bowl of lemon-infused water.

Pour the oil into a sauté dish and add the onions, carrot and garlic.

Sauté until soft and then add the artichokes, the white wine and the bouillon. Stir well, season with salt and pepper and add the herbs.

Cover and simmer gently for about 35 minutes.

With the addition of fried lardons this dish would be on its way to becoming the classic French dish, Artichokes Barigoule. Some chefs do not cut the artichokes in half but leave them whole. Their appearance reminds me of the curious Jewish hats found illustrated in medieval manuscripts.

ARTICHOKES, JERUSALEM

Jerusalem artichokes are a member of the sunflower family and were first found in North America. Their name is most likely to come from a corruption of the Italian for sunflower, girasole.

Jerusalem artichokes grow well in shady corners but do not thrive if left for too long in one spot. Trying to clear them can be arduous. A few scrubbed artichokes can be steamed along with new potatoes. To prepare boiled artichokes, I find it easier to peel off their skins after they are cooked.

Even the herbalist John Gerard (c. 1545-1612)
was aware of their side effects:

"Which way soever they be dressed and eaten,
they stir and cause a filthy loathsome stinking wind
within the body, thereby causing the belly to be
pained and tormented, and are a meal more
fit for swine than men."

Sautéed Artichokes

Peeled Jerusalem artichokes, gently fried in butter with salt and pepper. Lemon juice and parsley are added at the end. New potatoes can be included in this dish to make it more substantial.

Artichoke and Potato Soup

2 tbsp olive oil
2 medium onions, chopped
2 cloves garlic, crushed
350g Jerusalem artichokes, scrubbed and roughly chopped
350g potatoes, peeled and roughly chopped
1 litre chicken or vegetable stock
Juice of ½ lemon
Sprig of thyme
Salt and freshly ground black pepper

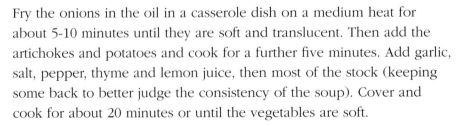

Fry the onions in the oil in a casserole dish on a medium heat for about 5-10 minutes until they are soft and translucent. Then add the artichokes and potatoes and cook for a further five minutes. Add garlic, salt, pepper, thyme and lemon juice, then most of the stock (keeping some back to better judge the consistency of the soup). Cover and cook for about 20 minutes or until the vegetables are soft.

Cool briefly, then purée the soup. Check consistency and seasoning.

Reheat before serving. A few drops of oil could be poured on the soup or a whirl of cream added to each bowl. Serve with croûtons.

ASPARAGUS

With luck the first asparagus appears in April just in time for the Grand National and we commemorate the Battle of Waterloo on 18 June with the last meal from our asparagus bed. It is then left to grow for the rest of the summer. The original bed must be over 25 years old and has been boosted by new plantings. We have no sure way of knowing the varieties we grow. It is given good coverings of manure or compost in the early spring and autumn and kept weed free.

When the spears are about six inches above ground, snap or cut them at the point where they cease to be tender. Do not cut any shoots that do not look bright or are straggly and, after the last picking, leave the bed until the autumn when the asparagus is tall and dry before cutting it down to the ground. Asparagus beetle can cause problems. Luckily, they are not only easy to see but also easy to catch.

Ignore asparagus pans, the best way to cook really fresh asparagus is to boil it gently in plenty of salted water for four to five minutes. A simple way to test the asparagus is to add a few of the woody ends cut off before cooking and test these. Asparagus spears are dense and continue to cook after having been taken from the heat. If cold asparagus is wanted, take it immediately from the pan and run it under cold water for several minutes. This not only stops further cooking but keeps the asparagus fresh looking.

Cheese, eggs and prosciutto are the natural partners for asparagus. For the simplest of meals, asparagus needs no more than butter and a little lemon juice.

Asparagus in a Salad of Pea Shoots

Dried peas, bought from a supermarket can be grown inside on porous paper kept moist with rain water. The shoots make a brilliant salad with thin slivers of raw asparagus, served with a simple vinaigrette dressing, topped with cubes of Feta cheese.

Chargrilled Asparagus

24 evenly matched asparagus spears
Olive oil
Salt and freshly ground black pepper

Heat a griddle pan. Brush the asparagus spears with oil and cook on the pan for about six minutes until lightly charred on all sides and just tender. Transfer to a plate, add a little more oil, salt and pepper.

This dish can be made more substantial by serving the asparagus topped with crumbled Feta cheese and a little more olive oil.

An alternative version is to roast asparagus in an oven (180°C). Fit asparagus spears in a single layer into a roasting dish. Add a little olive oil and turn the asparagus so that it is well coated. Sprinkle on a little salt and roast for about 15 minutes until tender.

LEMON BUTTER SAUCE FOR ASPARAGUS

A good sauce, less rich than Hollandaise and less challenging to make.

1 medium shallot, finely chopped
1 tbsp olive oil
250g unsalted butter, cubed
1 tbsp double cream or crème fraîche

1 glass white wine
1 lemon
Salt and freshly ground black pepper

Heat oil in a heavy saucepan, add the chopped shallot and cook gently for 3-4 minutes until soft. Add wine and juice of half the lemon. Cook until liquid is reduced by half. Add cream and cook for a further minute.

Remove from heat and whisk in the cubed butter until melted. Add the remaining lemon juice.

Sieve the liquid and, if not serving immediately, the sauce would keep well in a thermos flask.

ASPARAGUS WITH CREAM AND PASTA

450g fresh asparagus, woody ends
  removed, sliced at an angle into
  3cm lengths
50g unsalted butter
100ml double cream
100g Ricotta

Handful parsley, finely chopped
Pinch of nutmeg
Salt and freshly ground black pepper
Parmesan cheese, grated
350g penne or tagliatelle

Blanch the asparagus in boiling water for three minutes until almost cooked. Rinse in cold water and drain. In a saucepan, gently melt the butter. Add the cream and Ricotta, seasoning, nutmeg and asparagus and cook gently for about five minutes. Leave to one side while cooking the pasta.

When the pasta is cooked, drain and put back in the pan adding the asparagus sauce. Toss and serve with parsley and Parmesan scattered on top.

Asparagus Soup

A good way to use asparagus that are not of the best quality or shape but do not try to make soup from the woody stalks.

2 leeks, roughly chopped and washed
450g asparagus, roughly chopped
1 tbsp olive oil
1 litre vegetable stock
1 tbsp chopped chervil (or parsley)
2 tbsp double cream

Gently cook the leeks with the olive oil in a covered pan for 3-4 minutes until soft. Add the asparagus and vegetable stock. Bring to the boil, season lightly and simmer for about 10 minutes or until the asparagus is just soft enough to blend. Blend until smooth in a Liquidiser, then strain through a fine-meshed sieve. Check the seasoning. Pour into a saucepan. Add the cream and chervil (or parsley) and heat until almost boiling. Serve immediately.

CHINESE ASPARAGUS

These are a special treat.

Wrap asparagus spears, leaving their tips exposed, in a thin layer of filo pastry. (I find that one sheet cut into rectangles should be enough to wrap round eight spears.) Brush with egg and sprinkle with finely grated Parmesan cheese and sesame seeds.

Bake in a hot oven for 15-20 minutes or until the pastry is crisp and golden and the asparagus soft.

Serve while still warm, with soya sauce or the sauce in the recipe below.

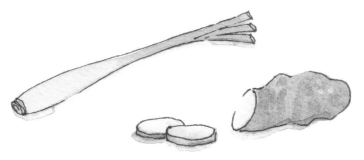

ORIENTAL SAUCE FOR ASPARAGUS

1 tsp finely chopped lemongrass bulb
1 tsp finely chopped root ginger
I tbsp Shaoxing rice wine (or dry sherry)
4 tbsp sunflower oil
Salt and freshly ground black pepper

Mix all the ingredients. Pour over
hot asparagus and serve.

PICKLED ASPARAGUS

Use these for a first course, served with smoked fish, prosciutto or a creamy cheese. They are so good that I make them again at Christmas with the freshest asparagus I can find, imported from Peru. Have ready a sterilised jar.

8-12 asparagus spears or as many as will fit upright into the jar
A mixture of $^2/_3$ white wine vinegar and $^1/_3$ white wine
   to fill the jar
1 tsp pickling spices
A few blades mace
Salt

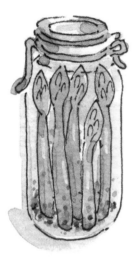

Prepare and wash the spears, then soak them in cold salted water for an hour or so. Drain and blanch in boiling water for two minutes. Drain and lay out to dry on a clean kitchen towel.

Simmer the vinegar and wine with the spices for 10 minutes. Allow to cool.

Carefully pack the spears into the jar, fill with the pickling liquid (including the spices), ensuring that the tips of the asparagus are covered, and seal.

The asparagus spears will keep fresh for up to two weeks in the fridge.

ASPARAGUS WITH CHOPPED HARD BOILED EGGS (ASPARAGUS MIMOSA)

I did not know the name for this delicious dish but am happy that Yotam Ottolenghi gives it its title, Asparagus Mimosa, in his book, *Plenty*. Like so many asparagus dishes, it is simple to prepare and delicious to eat. This is my version.

24 spears asparagus
3 eggs, hard boiled, peeled and chopped finely
Olive oil
2 tsp capers, drained
Salt and freshly ground black pepper

Trim the asparagus and cook for about four minutes until almost tender. (As in this dish the asparagus is served tepid, it will cook a little further in its own heat.) Dry the asparagus in kitchen paper and divide between four serving plates, adding just a hint of olive oil. Decorate with the capers, season generously with salt and pepper and finally add the chopped egg.

A perfect first course. Some might add Parmesan cheese or parsley to the dish but I do not think this necessary.

ASPARAGUS AND GOAT'S CHEESE TARTS

I like to make these deep tartlets using a six-hole muffin tin, but this recipe could also be used to make one 23cm diameter tart.

300g puff pastry (bought or home-made)
12 asparagus spears
3 eggs plus one yolk
100g soft goat's cheese
100g cream
Salt and freshly ground black pepper
Dusting of grated Parmesan cheese

Roll out the pastry and cut rounds to line the holes of the muffin tin. Place the pastry in the holes and put the tin in the fridge while preparing the filling.

Cook the asparagus in boiling water for four minutes. Cut off the tips the length of the diameter of the tarts and chop the remainder of the spears and divide them among the pastry tarts. Crumble the cheese and place this on top, then add the eggs, seasoned and whisked with the cream.

Finish with two spears laid on the top of each tart and sprinkle with the Parmesan cheese. Cook for 20 minutes or more at 180°C until the pastry is golden.

As the pastry has not been baked blind, it is best to give the bases of the tartlets extra heat by placing the tin on the floor of the oven for the last minutes of cooking.

Best served warm.

BROAD BEANS

I used to ride along the lanes near Compton Dando on my first horse, a huge thoroughbred called Balancer. From this height, I would admire the broad beans growing in one cottage garden. The gardener gladly gave his tip. Plant Aqua Dulce deep in a well manured bed during the last week of November. It was wise advice.

Broad beans are, along with peas, among the first vegetables to be cultivated and an early staple of the ancient world. There are various traditions associated with broad beans (or fava bean). Some Italians believe it is lucky to keep a bean in their pocket. The French cake, Galette des Rois, baked for the Christmas period and especially Epiphany, has a hidden bean nowadays often replaced by a trinket. The finder is made king! Certainly until late in the seventeenth century England had such a tradition and it continues in many parts of the world.

Broad beans have three ages, or four if you count the dried beans. Eat the young ones whole, sliced like green beans, then relish the small beans. Finally serve the large broad beans skinned and made into a purée. They are one of the few vegetables that freeze well.

BROAD BEANS AND PECORINO ANTIPASTI

Elizabeth David in *Italian Food*, 1954 so justly states: *'Among Italian Antipasti are to be found some of the most successful culinary achievements in European cooking'*. She rightly lists raw broad beans among possible ingredients. Young and sweet broad beans are perfect served with Pecorino cheese, perhaps some salami or Serrano ham and rustic bread.

FALAFEL

An Egyptian speciality that is traditionally made with dried broad beans. Broad beans, lightly cooked and then frozen work well in this recipe – making it a dish that can be served all year.

400g broad beans very lightly cooked, skinned if past their best
2 cloves garlic
½ tsp ground coriander
1½ tsp ground cumin
½ tsp ground chilli
3 spring onions
1 tbsp chopped parsley
1 tbsp chopped mint leaves
1 tbsp chopped coriander leaves
Salt and freshly ground black pepper
Groundnut oil for frying

Put the broad beans in the food processor with the garlic, ground coriander and cumin and blend to a coarse purée. Transfer to a bowl and mix in the green herbs, onions and seasoning. Shape into flattened balls (ping pong size), place on a tray and refrigerate for an hour.

Heat vegetable oil in a heavy bottomed pan or wok, fry the falafels in batches of four or five until golden brown on each side (five to six minutes). Drain on kitchen paper.

Serve with minted Greek yoghurt or as a starter with a herb salad and Feta cheese.

Mixed Beans with Spices

I love this dish, inspired by Yotam Ottolenghi. A particularly good recipe in which the strong taste of lovage is perfect. Celery leaves make a good substitute if no lovage is to hand.

3 tbsp olive oil
1 onion, finely chopped
2 cloves garlic, chopped
2 tsp tomato paste
½ tsp each ground cumin, ground coriander, and turmeric
1 tsp each ground ginger and cardamom
400g can chopped skinned tomatoes
125g mangetout or sugar snap peas, chopped at an angle
125g whole beans such as French beans or
    runner beans, chopped at an angle
250g shelled broad beans
1 tbsp lovage, finely chopped
Salt and freshly ground black pepper

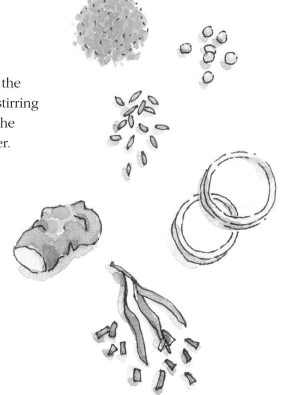

Heat the oil in a heavy pan, add the onion and sauté for a few minutes, stirring constantly. Add the garlic and then the tomato purée, spices, salt and pepper. Cook, continuing to stir for a further minute.

Add the tinned tomatoes with their juice, and all the peas and beans. Stir, then cover and cook gently for about 15 minutes until the largest peas are cooked but still retain some bite. Stir in the lovage leaves and serve warm or tepid.

Young Broad Beans cooked with Onion

This dish is one of the first delights of the year.

Trim young broad bean pods and cut them at an angle into lengths of about 2 cm. A few larger podded beans could also be added. Finely chop an onion and place it in a pan with a few tablespoons of olive oil, the beans and half a cup of water. Season lightly. Cover with a loose fitting lid and cook gently for about 15 minutes, stirring occasionally. A little liquid should be left in the bottom of the pan. This is the sauce in which the beans are served.

Broad Bean Purée

500g broad beans, boiled, retaining some of their cooking water
1 onion, roughly chopped
2 cloves garlic, crushed
2 tbsp olive oil
Juice of one lemon
½ tsp crushed chilli flakes
1 tsp ground coriander seeds
Salt and freshly ground black pepper

Skin the beans if they are old. Gently cook the onion in the olive oil until it is soft but not coloured. Add the crushed garlic, chilli flakes and then the broad beans. Season and cook for a few more minutes. Taste. Add lemon juice and transfer to blender to pulp, using a little of the retained water from the broad beans if necessary to get the right consistency.

This purée can be served warm with lamb dishes, on bruschetta, or used to make falafel.

RUNNER, FRENCH, BLUE LAKE
~ AND OTHER BEANS ~

There are so many sorts of beans. It is fun to grow new varieties but I would never want to be without runner beans. There is a special nostalgia at seeing the dying beans on the poles in the autumn.

BEAN SALAD

Lightly cooked prepared French beans tossed, while still warm, in a few tablespoons of olive oil and half the amount of white wine vinegar with a crushed clove of garlic, a little grain mustard, salt and freshly ground black pepper make a side dish to be served either tepid or cold.

A variation that goes well with cold roast beef is to simmer shallots in a little vinegar and water together with a teaspoon of grated horseradish. Mix a few tablespoons of the cooking liquid from the shallots with olive oil, salt and freshly ground black pepper to make the dressing. Mix the shallots and horseradish with the lightly cooked beans and add the dressing.

To serve with duck, mix warm French beans with crushed, lightly roasted hazelnuts, a little fine orange zest, crushed garlic, a few drops of orange juice and season.

CHINESE BEANS

In China they have beans that seem yards long but French beans or any beans that are not stringy are fine for this recipe.

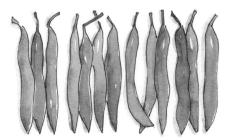

250g beans, trimmed
2 cloves garlic, finely chopped
Light sesame oil or groundnut oil
A pinch of chilli flakes
A little soya sauce

Pour a little oil into the wok and let it get hot. Tip in beans and stir actively for a minute. Add chilli flakes and garlic and continue to move the beans around for a further minute or two. Shake in a little soya sauce and add a little water (or, better, any available vegetable stock) if the beans need extra liquid. The thinnest beans should need no more than two more minutes to cook as it is important that they should keep some crispness.

BORLOTTI RATATOUILLE

This is essentially a peasant dish, but one that could brighten any mid-week dinner. If using dried beans, preparations for this dish are best started the night before.

1 large onion, skinned and finely chopped
3 tbsp olive oil
2 garlic cloves, finely chopped
2kg tomatoes, skinned and finely chopped
½ tsp chilli flakes
500g fresh borlotti beans (or 250g dried beans soaked overnight
  and cooked earlier in the day)
Salt and freshly ground black pepper
Generous bunch of coriander leaves, coarsely chopped

Gently cook the onion in most of the oil until soft but not coloured. Add the garlic, chilli flakes, and then the tomatoes and beans. Cover and leave to stew gently for about 45 minutes until all the ingredients are cooked and the sauce is thick. Season well. Before serving, add the coriander and remainder of the oil.

BORLOTTI BEAN BRUSCHETTA

Cooked borlotti beans, perhaps leftover from a bean stew, crushed and put on hot bread that has been rubbed with garlic. Pour a few drops of olive oil over the beans and then top with ground black pepper and chopped parsley to make a light lunch.

RUNNER BEAN CHUTNEY

This makes the best chutney for Boxing Day as it goes so well with cold poultry. I am grateful to Margaret Kelland for introducing me to this recipe. I have since discovered that it has a great following. Over the years, this has become my version.

750g runner beans	2 tsp grain mustard
2 medium onions	1 tsp ground allspice
150ml distilled malt vinegar	2 tsp turmeric
1 tsp coriander seed	150ml cider vinegar
1 tsp yellow mustard seed	200g granulated sugar
1 tsp fenugreek seed	1 generous tsp salt
1 tbsp English mustard	250g tomatoes
powder	30g corn flour

String the beans, removing the stalks. Thinly slice each bean, cutting diagonally to give fine shreds about 4 or 5cm long. Bring a pan of water to the boil, add the beans and let boil for a minute before straining and leaving to cool in the colander.

Peel and finely chop the onions, put them into a medium-sized saucepan with the malt vinegar, coriander, yellow mustard seeds, and fenugreek seeds. Bring to the boil then lower the heat and let simmer for 10 minutes.

Mix the remaining mustards, allspice, turmeric, sugar, salt and half the cider vinegar in a small basin. Dice the tomatoes (no need to skin them) then add to the vinegar and onions, stir in the beans and mustard mixture. Simmer for five minutes. Make a smooth paste with the remaining cider vinegar and corn flour and add this. Let the chutney cook for a further 10 minutes, stirring often, until the sauce has thickened.

Poor into sterilized jars and store for at least a month before serving.

BEETROOT

As a child, boiled beetroot doused in malt vinegar filled me with horror. It is a puzzle that so many good recipes for beetroot were overlooked by at least one generation. The small, sweet beetroot we grow have made me a convert. Beetroot goes especially well with allspice, thyme, apples, horseradish, yoghurt or soured cream sauce.

"The greater red Beet or Roman Beet, boyled and eaten with oyle, vinegre and pepper, is a most excellent and delicat sallad; but what might be made of the red and beautifull root (which is to be preferred before the leaves, as well in beautie as in goodnesse) I refer unto the curious and cunning cooke, who no doubt when hee had the view therof, and is assured that it is both good and wholesome, will make therof many and divers dishes, both faire and good."

John Gerard,
Herball or *Generall Historie of Plantes*,
3rd ed. 1636.

BORSCHT

There are any numbers of soups to be made using beetroot. Borscht is the most famous and even this soup can be very varied. It is essential, however, to use good beef stock. I prefer a lighter borscht.

1 litre good quality beef stock
2 raw beetroot, grated
250g minced beef
Whites and shells of two eggs
1 glass sherry
Salt

Put the beef stock into a pan together with the grated beetroot, minced beef and egg whites, lightly whipped to a froth. Add the egg shells, cleaned and crushed. Over a low heat, whisk the liquid until it starts to boil. Let the liquid rise in the pan before drawing it to one side. Leave to settle and then return to a gentle heat and let simmer for 30 minutes. Taste the consommé and season. Allow to cool and strain through a cloth.

To serve, reheat the borscht, add the sherry and serve with sour cream and perhaps some snipped chives. Piroshki are traditionally served with borscht.

BEETROOT WITH ALLSPICE

A recipe inspired by Elizabeth David and my favourite way of serving beetroot.

Cook raw beetroot, the size of golf balls, in boiling water until tender. Plunge into cold water, then peel. While still warm, quarter the beets, season with salt and pepper and ground allspice. Add a little olive oil and white wine vinegar. Mix the beetroot in the dressing and leave to cool before serving.

GREEK BEETROOT SALAD

A good salad in which the beetroot leaves are also used. In Greece it is cooked as a Lenten dish.

4-5 medium sized beetroot
1 tbsp capers
3 tbsp olive oil
1 tbsp red wine vinegar
1 tbsp balsamic vinegar
Salt and freshly ground black pepper

Separate the leaves from the roots and put the best, including their stalks, to one side. Wash the beetroot and cook them in salted water.

Wash the leaves and stalks and then chop them roughly. After the beetroot has been cooking for 30 minutes, add the leaves and stalks to the boiling water.

Allow to cook for a few minutes more. Drain. Take out the beetroot and, when cool enough to handle, skin them and chop them into wedges. Turn the leaves and stalks into a bowl, adding the beetroot wedges, capers, oil and vinegars and seasoning.

Serve at room temperature.

THYME-ROASTED BEETROOT

6 even-sized beetroot
6 whole cloves garlic
Salt
Olive oil
Fresh thyme

Take off the tops and wash the beetroot leaving the skin intact.
Quarter and arrange the beetroot segments in a roasting tin with the
garlic cloves, skinned. Add a little olive oil and turn the segments in
it, so that they are all coated. Scatter over the thyme leaves, salt and
roast in a preheated oven (180°-190°C) for 35-40 minutes or until
beetroot is cooked.

BEETROOT BOURGUIGNON

1 large red onion, finely sliced
4 tbsp olive oil
3 cloves garlic, chopped
8 small beetroot, peeled and quartered
6 carrots, sliced at an angle into pieces about 3cm long
3 bay leaves
Small bunch thyme
2 tbsp tomato paste
150 ml red wine
100 ml vegetable stock
Salt and freshly ground black pepper

A good winter dish. Heat the oil in a large casserole pot. Add the onions
and sauté until soft. Add the garlic, beetroot, carrots and let cook for about
two minutes. Then add wine, stock, and tomato purée. Keeping the thyme
in a bunch, also add the herbs and season. Cover and cook in a moderate
oven (170°C) for about 45 minutes. Test the beetroot and carrots to
make sure they are fully cooked and season.Serve with Puy lentils.

Beetroot Relish

500g beetroot
500g onions
2 tbsp fresh grated horseradish
1 tbsp salt
1 tbsp powdered mustard
1 tsp white ground pepper
250g granulated sugar
600 ml white wine vinegar
1 tbsp pickling spices in a muslin spice bag (optional)

Boil the beetroot in the usual way until cooked. Skin and chop roughly into small pieces. Put into a preserving pan together with the onion, finely chopped, horseradish and half the vinegar. Cook until the onions are soft. Mix the mustard in a little of the remaining vinegar. Add this to the pan with the rest of the vinegar, sugar, pickling spices (if using) and the salt and pepper. Simmer the relish, checking it often, for about 40 minutes until it is the right consistency. Turn up the heat for the last five minutes of cooking. Remove the spice bag, if used.

Pour into clean jars with tight fitting lids. Allow flavours to mature for a month before opening and, once opened, store jars in the fridge.

Pickled Beetroot

An excellent way to use thinnings.

Boil small beetroot in water until tender. In a separate pan, boil sufficient white wine vinegar to pickle the beets to which has been added, depending on quantities and taste, approximately $^1/_2$ teaspoon cayenne pepper, one teaspoon ground ginger and a few black peppercorns.

When the beets are cool, peel them and put them into prepared jars. Top up with the cooled spiced vinegar and seal.

BEETROOT AND CHOCOLATE CAKE

For the cake:
3 beetroot,
300g caster sugar
3 eggs
250g butter
250g self-raising flour
75g cocoa powder
1 tbsp bicarbonate of soda

For the filling:
100g butter
1 tbsp cocoa powder
2 tbsp icing sugar
2 tbsp milk
2 tbsp cherry jam

The oven temperature is 180°C.

Cook the beetroot in boiling water, skin them and grate coarsley.

Prepare two 20cm cake tins by buttering them and lining them with baking parchment.

Cream the butter and sugar and then add the beaten eggs, cocoa, beetroot and sift in the flour and bicarbonate of soda. Mix well and divide mixture between the two cake tins. Cook for about 35 minutes or until cakes are springy to the touch. Let the cakes stand for a few minutes before inverting them carefully onto a wire rack to cool.

To make the butter cream filling, sift the icing sugar with the cocoa, beat in the softened butter and, still beating, add the milk drop by drop until the right consistency is achieved.

Spread the filling on one flat side of one cake and the cherry jam on the other. Sandwich them together and, finally, dust some icing sugar over the top.

BROCCOLI

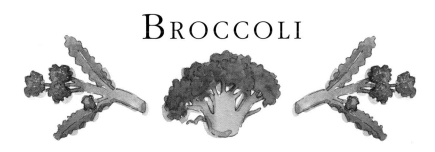

Poor broccoli; in 1990 President George Bush's public dislike of the vegetable caused a crisis for American broccoli growers. Luckily allotment owners know better. We may not grow big round calabrese but simply boiled purple sprouting broccoli is a treat for late winter, served with a little olive oil and squeeze of lemon juice or lightly roasted with olive oil and put on top of a Stilton cheese and caper bruschetta.

Broccoli even has a whole new life used raw in smoothies. Any number of other ingredients can be added – oats, blueberries, peanuts, bananas, raisins, honey, maple syrup – blended with soya, almond milk or yoghurt to give a nutritious drink.

BROCCOLI AND STILTON SOUP

This is a great soup in which to use the last vestiges of the Christmas Stilton. Other blue cheeses such as Bath Blue or Gorgonzola can be mixed in or used in place of the Stilton. A spoonful of plain Philadelphia cheese could also be added to good effect.

350g purple sprouting broccoli
30g butter
1 onion, peeled and roughly chopped
1 medium potato
1 clove garlic
1 litre chicken or game stock
50 ml full fat milk
50ml single cream
125g Stilton or another creamy blue cheese
Salt and freshly ground black pepper

Prepare the broccoli, by cutting off the toughest stems or leaves and chopping the rest into chunks.

Melt the butter in a large heavy bottomed saucepan and add the onion. Gently fry for a few minutes, then add the potato and garlic. Continue frying for about five minutes, not letting the vegetables colour, then add the broccoli and stock. Stir and bring to the boil, then cover and simmer for 10-15 minutes until the vegetables are tender.

Take from the heat and add the cheese. When cool enough, purée the soup in a food processor and then pass it through a sieve. If you do not do this, any stringy bits are sure to catch you out.

Return the soup to the saucepan and add milk and cream, more or less depending on how thick you want the soup. Check for seasoning and bring the soup to the point of boiling before serving.

Salad of Calabrese Stalks

Tender stalks of calabrese make a delightful salad. Put stalks that have been peeled and cut into uniform lengths into a jar. Add a dressing made from 2:1 olive oil to sherry vinegar, a generous pinch of salt, and a clove of crushed garlic. Seal the jar, give it a good shake and store in the fridge. Use within 24 hours.

Purple Sprouting Broccoli with Pickled Walnuts and Pecorino Cheese

This is my favourite way of serving broccoli. The walnuts give sharpness and the cheese sweetness. It makes an excellent first course served with toast and is a great accompaniment to grilled chicken or escalopes. I have also served it with turkey burgers after Christmas when the Pecorino cheese was replaced by Stilton.

400g purple sprouting broccoli
A jar of pickled walnuts, drained and chopped
4 tbsp olive oil
60g butter
Salt and freshly ground black pepper
80g Pecorino cheese

Cook the broccoli in boiling salted water for about five minutes or until tender. Drain well and return to the pan. On a low heat, add the butter and stir until melted. Arrange on a serving dish. Mix the pickled walnuts with the olive oil and spoon over the broccoli. Add slivers of cheese.

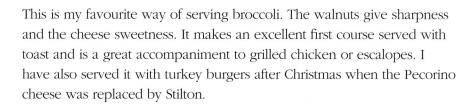

BROCCOLI WITH PASTA

❋

This dish has endless variations. Common to all is to cook the penne and boil or steam the broccoli and then mix them together in a baking dish before adding the sauce which may or may not require cooking. I give recipes for two sauces.

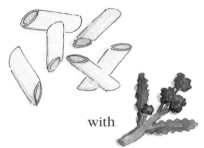

300g penne
350g purple sprouting or any broccoli

Cream sauce

250 ml double cream or cream mixed   with
  marscapone
125g semi-dried tomatoes, chopped
Salt and freshly ground black pepper
Grated Parmesan cheese

Mix the sauce ingredients and pour over the cooked broccoli and pasta. Top with some grated Parmesan. Bake at 180°C for 20 minutes or until the top is browned and bubbling.

Anchovy Sauce

6-8 tomatoes, skinned, deseeded, and chopped
1 tin anchovies in oil
1 small onion, peeled and finely chopped
1 clove garlic
½ tsp chilli flakes
Salt and freshly ground black pepper

Put the anchovies and their oil in a frying pan and add the onion. Fry gently for about five minutes or until the onion is soft. Add the garlic and chilli flakes and then the tomatoes. Cook for a few minutes more. Season well before pouring over the cooked pasta and broccoli. Bake as above. Stoned black olives could be added if some are to hand.

BRUSSELS SPROUTS

Unsung heroes! Delicious if only they are steamed or boiled for as long as it takes to carve the roast.

*"These delicate little
sprouts, or miniature cabbages,
which at their fullest growth scarcely
exceed a large walnut in size, should be quite
freshly gathered. Free them from all discoloured
leaves, cut the stems even, and wash the sprouts
thoroughly. Throw them into a pan of water properly
salted, and boil them quickly from eight to ten minutes;
drain them well, and serve them upon a rather thick round
of toasted bread buttered on both sides. Send good melted
butter to table with them. This is the Belgian mode of
dressing this excellent vegetable, which is served in France
with the sauce poured over it, or it is tossed in a stewpan
with a slice of butter and some pepper and salt: a
spoonful or two of veal gravy (and sometimes a
little lemon-juice) is added when these are
perfectly mixed."*

Eliza Acton,
*Modern Cookery
for Private Families,*
1845

BRUSSELS SPROUTS WITH CHESTNUTS

Steam or boil the prepared Brussels sprouts for five minutes. Add chestnut pieces (from chestnuts that have been simmered for about 10 minutes and skinned) and cook for a further two minutes. Drain and serve, tossed with a little butter. Perfect with the Christmas turkey.

Any leftovers could be puréed and made into a sauce

BRUSSELS SPROUTS WITH MUSTARD

This recipe was a lucky find. It was overheard being discussed by my daughter while on a bus in New York.

500g Brussels sprouts
2 tbs olive oil
1 tsp moutarde de Meaux
a few strips pancetta chopped (optional)

Steam the Brussels sprouts for about five minutes until almost cooked. Heat olive oil in a wide pan and add the drained sprouts and then the mustard. Cook, tossing the sprouts around for a minute then add the pancetta and cook a further minute.

CABBAGE

Cabbage was banned from my childhood home; such was the phobia of my father from his childhood experience. It is a great pity that my mother didn't try some disguised inventiveness. For me it remains a great treat.

Cabbage is one of the oldest and most widely used green vegetables. Sea cabbage still grows naturally along our coast and would have been used in the Dark Ages. In 17th and 18th century Europe, cabbage was the staple food from England to Russia and into the Eastern Mediterranean. The Far East knew cabbage too. The Koreans have their legendary dish, kimchi, in which fermented cabbage is the main ingredient. In China white cabbage is used in many dishes including their festive dumplings.

We would have eaten very much more cabbage during the two World Wars. Old photographs of allotment sites show how much was grown. Despite its popularity, cabbage does attract a wide variety of pests and is not a failsafe crop.

EVERYDAY CABBAGE

Remove the outer leaves of a cabbage, then core it and slice any large veins. Chop the cabbage and boil it gently in salted water until the leaves are soft and the veins tender. Test by trying some of the larger veins. Strain, return to the pan with a good knob of butter and warm through. Grind black pepper over the cabbage before serving.

MANGO COLESLAW

With an Indian flavour, this is a refreshing alternative to coleslaw.

1 tbsp coriander seeds
1 tbsp cumin seeds
¼ white cabbage
1 large carrot, peeled and coarsely grated
1 slightly under-ripe mango, peeled
    and coarsely grated
2 handfuls coriander leaves, roughly chopped
Juice of 2 limes
2 tbsp sunflower oil
Salt and freshly ground black pepper

Dry fry the coriander and cumin seeds in a frying pan for about a minute until they crackle, turn brown and give off scent. Grind these to a fine powder in a mortar.

Take out the core of the cabbage and slice the rest very finely. In a large bowl, mix all the ingredients and serve immediately.

CHINESE STIR FRIED CABBAGE

1 large green cabbage
3 tbsp vegetable oil
1 red chilli, deseeded and chopped
1 clove garlic, crushed
Pinch of salt
A little vegetable stock (potato water would be perfect)
Light soya sauce

Wash the cabbage and take off the outer tough leaves and the core. Quarter it and slice the sections into thin strips. Heat oil in a wok until hot, put in the chopped chilli, the garlic and then the cabbage and stir for one minute until the cabbage softens. Then add salt and a little stock to encourage the juice the cabbage is already releasing. Keep stirring for about three minutes and then shake in about two tablespoons of soya sauce before serving.

ITALIAN CABBAGE

For variety, using the above recipe but preferring a Savoy cabbage, smoked bacon or lardons could be cooked along with the chilli. Omit the soya sauce.

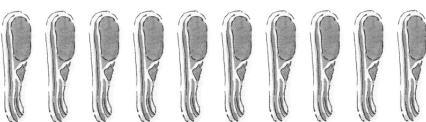

RED CABBAGE WITH PEARS

Based on the recipe in *The Cuisine of Hungary* by George Lang.

125g smoked lardons or finely chopped smoked bacon
1 large onion, chopped
1 firm red cabbage, core removed and finely sliced
2 cloves garlic, crushed
1 tsp caraway seeds
1 tsp salt
½ tsp freshly ground black pepper
2 ripe pears peeled, cored and chopped
1 lemon, halved
1 glass red wine
3 tbsp red wine vinegar
3 tbsp honey

Brown the lardons (or bacon) in a heavy pot until golden. Add the chopped onion and let the mixture cook gently until the onion turns blond and gives off juice. Add the cabbage, garlic, caraway seeds, and a little water. Cover, and cook until the cabbage starts to soften.

Add the salt, pepper, and then the pears, lemon halves, red wine and vinegar. Cook, covered, for 15 minutes and then add the honey.

From now on, cook on a very low heat, or in the oven at about 130°C. Check from time to time. If the cabbage is beginning to dry out, add a little more water. If the cabbage is 'swimming' take off the lid and let enough of the liquid steam away.

This dish can take an hour or more to cook. It is even better if cooked the day before it is to be eaten and reheated carefully.

Remove the lemon halves before serving.

CARROTS

In a radio interview I remember Clarissa Dickson-Wright admitting to not liking carrots. I sympathize. Young fresh carrots have little in common with the slimy stale versions so often found wrapped to suffocation in supermarkets. Raw grated carrots in a mayonnaise dressing with either celery or celeriac are welcome as a winter salad or, sliced at a slant, and added to a mixture of roasted winter vegetables. Carrots added to tomato soup gives depth to the flavour and a sliced carrot in a beef marinade does unexplainable wonders.

Carrots need good sandy soil. Planted in fresh manure, they are likely to fork or become baroque.

"Sow carrots in your gardens and humbly praise God for them, as for a singular and great blessing."

Richard Gardner,
Profitable Instructions for the Manuring, Sowing and Planting of Kitchen Gardens, 1599

EVERYDAY CARROTS

With a potato peeler, peel older carrots, trim and cut into batons. Young carrots could be left whole. Cook in a little water with a good lump of butter. Check from time to time to make sure the water hasn't evaporated until the carrots are cooked and then let it evaporate. The carrots can fry in the butter for the last minute or two of cooking, turning a little brown on some edges. Pour over a little lemon juice and sprinkle with chopped parsley.

PENNY'S CARROT AND SPINACH TERRINE

450g spinach

900g carrots

2 ripe avocados

3-4 cloves garlic

25g powdered gelatine

4 tbsp white wine vinegar

6 tbsp olive oil

2-3 tsp mustard powder

2 tsp caster sugar

A little grated nutmeg

Salt and black pepper

Boil the spinach leaves in salted water for a minute, then drain and spread out on clean tea towels or kitchen paper to dry.

Peel and chop carrots and boil with unpeeled garlic cloves until tender. Drain, reserving 500ml of the water. When cold, blend them with the garlic cloves pressed out of their skins.

Oil a 23cm paté terrine and line it with three quarters of the spinach leaves, making sure that the top ones overlap the sides of the dish.

Carefully dissolve the gelatine in the reserved carrot water, making sure that no lumps remain. Tip the purée mixture into the gelatine, add the vinegar, oil, mustard, sugar, nutmeg and season to taste. Pour half the carrot mixture into the terrine, lay thin slices of avocado on top and then pour over the rest. Fold in the remaining spinach leaves. Refrigerate for a few hours before turning out, slicing and serving.

CARROT SALAD WITH CHILLI

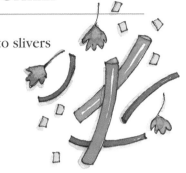

4 medium carrots, trimmed, peeled and sliced into slivers
1 medium-sized red chilli, thinly sliced
A little root ginger, peeled and finely chopped
A little fresh coriander
3 tbsp rice wine vinegar
1 tbsp caster sugar

Mix the sugar with the vinegar. In a bowl, combine all the other ingredients and pour over the vinegar. Leave no more than an hour before serving. Good served with cold beef.

CARROT AND CUMIN SALAD

A surprisingly simple but interesting salad, best served with a meze. This was inspired by a recipe in *The Independent* by Mark Hix.

500g medium carrots
Juice of 1 orange
Vegetable stock
3 tsp cumin seeds
Salt and freshly ground black pepper
3 tbsp olive oil
Juice of 1 lemon
Handful chopped coriander

Peel the carrots with a potato peeler. Slice on an angle as thinly as possible, preferably using a mandoline. Cook them for 8-10 minutes in a covered saucepan with the orange juice, cumin seeds, salt and just enough stock to cover. Drain, but keep the liquid which continues to cook until reduced to 3-4 tablespoons. Allow to cool.

Put the carrots in a bowl with the olive oil and lemon juice. Add enough of the reduced stock to the carrots to complete the dressing. Season and add the chopped coriander.

CARROT CAKE WITH LIME MASCARPONE ICING

285g salted butter, softened

285g light brown soft sugar

5 eggs, separated

Zest and juice of 1 orange

170g self-raising flour, sifted

1 slightly heaped teaspoon baking powder

115g ground almonds

115g shelled walnuts, chopped, plus
 a handful for decorating

1 heaped teaspoon ground cinnamon

A pinch of ground cloves

A pinch of ground nutmeg

½ tsp ground ginger

285g carrots, peeled and coarsely grated

A pinch of salt

For the icing:

115g mascarpone cheese

225g full fat cream cheese

85g icing sugar, sifted

Zest and juice of 2 limes

Oven at 180°C. Grease and line a 22cm square cake tin or a round equivalent with greaseproof paper. Beat the butter and sugar together until pale and fluffy. Beat in the egg yolks one at a time and add the orange zest and juice. Stir in the sifted flour and baking powder, and add the ground almonds, walnuts, spices and grated carrot and mix together well.

In a separate bowl, whisk the egg whites with a pinch of salt until stiff, and then gently fold them into the cake mix. Scoop the mixture into the prepared cake tin and cook in the preheated oven for about 50 minutes until golden and risen. Leave the cake to cool in the tin for 10 minutes, then turn it out on to a rack and leave for at least an hour.

Mix all the icing ingredients together and spread generously over the top of the cake.

Finish off with a sprinkling of chopped walnuts.

CAULIFLOWER

Unlike my allotment neighbours, I have not been very successful at growing cauliflower. How strange it is that what one person can grow successfully another fails and the plots are only a few steps apart. I remember a weekend in Normandy, staying in Roscoff and travelling no further than we could walk from the ferry. We passed small plots neatly filled with cauliflowers and artichokes. English cauliflowers are at their best early in the winter.

Cauliflower is perhaps the most difficult of vegetables to cook. Cooked too much it becomes mushy, too little and it is hard. If cooking the head whole, it is wise to cut a cross at the bottom of the stem to prevent the florets from over cooking before the centre is soft. A bay leaf in the water of a boiling cauliflower reduces its smell. A little Dijon mustard added to a white sauce much improves the traditional dish and most cauliflower recipes omit pepper.

Indian and Middle Eastern cooking give a new dimension to cauliflower. Cumin, coriander and turmeric are its most complementary spices. Roasted pine nuts, hazelnuts and raisins can be sprinkled on top to give variations.

Roasted Cauliflower and Hazelnut Salad

As I write this (on the eve of Thanksgiving 2013) New York seems to be in the grip of a roasted cauliflower salad explosion, caused by the US publication of Yotam Ottolenghi's splendid book, *Jerusalem*. It is truly delicious and fantastic to serve as a first course or with a spiced roasted chicken.

1 cauliflower head, divided into small florets
5 tbsp olive oil
1 large stick of celery, cut at an angle into thin slices
30g hazelnuts
10g flat leaf parsley leaves
50g pomegranate seeds
½ tsp ground cinnamon
½ tsp ground allspice
1 tbsp sherry vinegar
1½ tsp maple syrup
Salt and freshly ground black pepper

Mix the cauliflower with about half the olive oil and some salt and black pepper and spread out on a roasting tin. Roast at about 220°C for 25-35 minutes or until the cauliflower is crisp and parts are turning brown. Transfer to a large mixing bowl and set aside to cool.

Spread the hazelnuts on a baking tray lined with parchment and roast at 170°C for 17 minutes (Ottolenghi's precise timing is accurate).

Allow the hazelnuts to cool, then chop them and add them to the cauliflower with the rest of the ingredients. Stir, taste and serve at room temperature.

EVERYDAY INDIAN CAULIFLOWER AND POTATOES

1 cauliflower, cut into florets
250g potatoes, peeled and diced
4 tbsp vegetable oil
1 tsp cumin seeds
1 tbsp ground coriander
1 tsp turmeric
½ tsp chilli flakes
250g tomatoes, skinned and chopped
Salt
Coriander leaves, chopped

Put the oil into a large frying pan and, when it is hot, add the cumin seeds. Fry for about half a minute or until they are dark brown, then add all the other spices (it is wise to have them all measured and ready for use), the cauliflower and potatoes. Fry for five minutes or so until the vegetables start to colour. Add the tomatoes.

Add a few tablespoons of water and the salt. Cover and let the vegetables cook gently for about 15 minutes or until they are tender and cooked through. Check them from time to time to be sure that there is enough water.

Serve sprinkled with chopped coriander leaves.

Peas can be added to this dish to good effect. If using frozen peas, they need only be added in the last five minutes of cooking. Yoghurt can be used in place of the tomatoes, stirred in at the end of cooking.

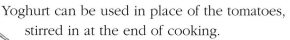

PICCALILLI

½ cauliflower, cut into tiny florets
1 large onion, chopped
6 shallots, peeled and quartered
1 carrot, peeled and diced into
   small pieces
½ cucumber, deseeded and cut
   into 1 cm dice
1½ tbsp sea salt

1½ tbsp cornflour
300ml cider vinegar
200ml malt vinegar
175g caster sugar
1 tbsp English mustard powder
1 tbsp turmeric
2 red chillies, deseeded and thinly
   sliced

Put the cauliflower, onion, shallots, carrot, and cucumber in a large bowl. Add the salt, mix well, cover and leave overnight.

The next day, rinse the vegetables thoroughly and drain them, then dry them with kitchen towel.

In a basin, mix the cornflour with some of the vinegar until it is smooth and the consistency of single cream. Put the rest of the vinegars, sugar, turmeric, mustard and chillies in a preserving pan and stir over a medium heat until the sugar has dissolved.

Bring to the boil and add the vegetables. Simmer for five minutes, then remove from the heat and stir in the cornflour.

Return to the heat and, stirring constantly, let the mixture boil gently for about three minutes or until the sauce is thick.

Pour into sterilized jars and seal. Leave for six weeks in a cool place before using. Once opened, store in the fridge and use within four weeks.

CAVOLO NERO AND KALE

Cavolo nero is a relative newcomer to the English kitchen garden. It is great not only for its taste and versatility but also its convenience; as much as is needed can be picked, leaving more leaves on the stalk. Little white flies can attack it but do no real damage. They are easily dispelled with a good shake and wash. The tough, bottom end of the stalks should be removed before cooking.

Kale is less kindly regarded. *'Dig for Victory'* and Scottish broths come to mind. Allotment holders, by picking young stalks, know how good steamed kale can taste. Russian kale is a spiky newcomer with a more peppery taste than normal kale. It can be cooked in the usual way but also deep fried to look like seaweed and used to accompany smoked fish.

COLCANNON

This classic kale dish, delicious served with baked ham, is the bubble and squeak of Ireland.

500g potatoes, peeled
200g leeks, sliced
300g kale, stalks removed, then chopped
Butter
Milk
Salt and freshly ground black pepper

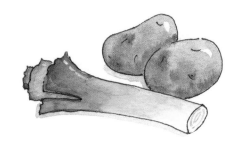

Boil the potatoes until soft. Mash them carefully making sure no lumps remain and add butter and milk to make a light mashed potato. Season well.

Fry the leeks gently in butter until soft and steam the kale for a few minutes until cooked.

Keep all three elements warm and combine them together in a dish before serving.

Colcannon also works well using crumbly new potatoes. Omit the milk but use plenty of butter.

Ribollita

Cavolo nero is essential for this Tuscan rustic soup which is said to date from the Middle Ages when servants would use stale bread to soak up vegetable gravy left from their master's table. Cooking needs to be started a day in advance with the dried beans.

200g prepared cannellini or borlotti beans (or tins could be substituted)
Olive oil
1 onion, peeled and chopped
1 large bunch flat leafed parsley, chopped
2 whole heads celery, chopped
4 cloves garlic, peeled and chopped
400g carrots, peeled and finely chopped
400g ripe tomatoes, peeled, deseeded, and chopped
2kg cavolo nero, stalks removed and chopped
1 litre vegetable stock
1 ciabatta loaf, one day old
Salt and freshly ground black pepper

Put about four tablespoons of olive oil in a large saucepan and gently fry the onion, parsley, celery and carrot for about 30 minutes until the vegetables are soft. Add the garlic and tomatoes and cook, with the lid on, for another 20 minutes. Then add the cavolo nero and half the beans and continue cooking gently.

Purée the remaining beans with some of their liquid. Add to the soup with enough water or vegetable stock to give the soup the right consistency. Break the ciabatta loaf into small pieces and add to the soup together with salt, pepper and a shake of olive oil.

Grated Parmesan cheese can be served with this soup.

Cavolo Nero Sauce for Penne

300g penne
500g cavolo nero, stalks removed and roughly chopped
3 cloves garlic, skinned and chopped
100g pine nuts, lightly toasted
60 ml or more olive oil
Salt and freshly ground black pepper
Parmesan or Pecorino cheese

Cook the cavolo nero in a large pan of salted water. Drain well but retain a little of the water. Put the cavolo nero into a blender together with the pine nuts and garlic. Blend very briefly (you may need to add some of the cooking water to get it to 'move') and then add 60ml olive oil for the last seconds of blitzing to make a rough, dark green, loose pesto. Season to taste.

Keep the sauce warm in a saucepan while the pasta is cooking.

When the penne are cooked, drain thoroughly and put them into the sauce, stirring well so that each piece is coated. A little more olive oil could now be added to give extra gloss. Serve with Parmesan or sliced Pecorino cheese.

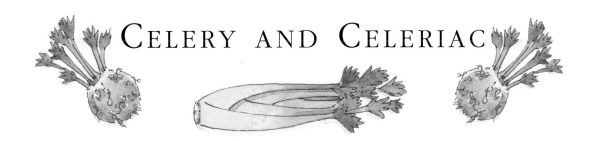

CELERY AND CELERIAC

In truth, the celery we grow on the allotment is nothing like that grown in the peaty soil of East Anglia. Nevertheless, the leaves can be used to flavour soups and can be chopped fine and added to chicken casseroles. Even East Anglian celery can be stringy. Never skimp on sieving or chopping.

Celery is wonderful with walnuts in a Waldorf salad or made into a sandwich with Cheddar cheese. It makes the best 'swizzle stick' for a Bloody Mary. I use one stick, finely chopped, in Bolognese sauce or in creamy chicken casseroles. Best, I like celery flavoured with coriander. A teaspoon of white wine vinegar sharpens the flavour of cooked celery.

Celeriac is such a versatile vegetable, an unsung hero. Mashed with butter, made into a gratin, puréed with potatoes or Bramley apples to serve with roast duck, grated and mixed with carrots in coleslaw, it has a myriad of uses mostly in conjunction with other vegetables. Never be tempted to Liquidise celeriac for use as a purée; it ruins the texture, making it watery.

Peri: Doctor, why do you wear a stick of celery in your lapel?

The Doctor: Does it offend you?

Peri: No, just curious.

The Doctor: Safety precaution. I'm allergic to certain gases in the praxis range of the spectrum.

Peri: Well, how does the celery help?

The Doctor: If the gas is present, the celery turns purple.

Peri: And then what do you do?

The Doctor: I eat the celery. If nothing else, I'm sure it's good for my teeth.

Dr Who, *March 1984*

Braised Celery Hearts

Braising suits celery. This is a dish that goes well with chicken or duck.

Celery hearts well-trimmed and quartered, first cooked gently in salted water for five minutes and then braised, barely covered, in chicken stock with a tablespoon of white wine vinegar for about 1½ hours until the sauce is reduced almost to a syrup.

A variation would be to replace the chicken stock and vinegar with skinned tomatoes and flavoured with coriander seeds and leaves.

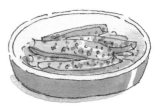

Cream of Celery Soup

50g butter
350g celery, cleaned and chopped
1 onion, peeled and chopped
1 large potato, peeled and
  chopped

1 litre chicken stock
150 ml single cream (or
  mascarpone)
Salt and freshly ground white
  pepper

Melt the butter in a pan and gently cook the onions and celery until soft but not coloured. Add the potato, the stock and salt and bring to boil. Cover and allow to cook for about 35 minutes. Liquidise and then pass through a sieve to be sure no stringy bits remain. Return to the pan, add cream and pepper. Allow to heat but not boil and serve with croûtons.

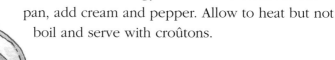

CELERIAC AND THYME GRATIN

700g celeriac, peeled
1 tbsp lemon juice
500 ml double cream
1 clove garlic
½ tsp freshly grated nutmeg
Handful of thyme leaves
25g Parmesan cheese, grated
Salt and freshly ground black pepper
Butter for greasing

Grease a gratin dish. Slice the celeriac to the thickness of a coin and put it in a bowl of cold water with the lemon juice. In a large bowl mix the cream, garlic, nutmeg and most of the thyme. Drain the celeriac and add to the cream mixture. Season well.

Lay the celeriac and sauce into the gratin dish. Cover with foil and cook in a hot oven (190°C) for 45 minutes. Uncover, sprinkle with the cheese and remaining thyme and cook for a further 15 minutes or so until the top is lightly browned and the celeriac soft when pierced with a sharp knife.

Classic Rémoulade

1 medium-sized celeriac	3-4 tbsp mayonnaise, either bought
1 lemon	or home-made (see page 212)
1 tin anchovies in oil (optional)	1 tbsp yoghurt
2 tbsp capers	2 tbsp parsley, finely chopped
	Salt and freshly ground black pepper

Peel the celeriac and either grate coarsely or slice thinly and then cut the slices into matchsticks. By using a food processor or mandoline there are any number of ways of achieving this end. As you work, to prevent the slices turning brown, put them into a bowl of water acidulated with lemon juice.

Mix the mayonnaise with the yoghurt. Drain the celeriac and pat dry with a tea towel. Put into a bowl and stir in the mayonnaise dressing. Add the anchovies, if using, drained of oil and chopped, the capers and parsley. Mix carefully and season before serving.

Indian Celeriac Rémoulade

An excellent dish to serve with kebabs, meatballs or as a starter. Instead of mixing spices, two teaspoons of the Indian spice mix, panch phoram, could be substituted.

1 medium-sized celeriac	Olive oil
1 lemon	2 tsp blend of whole spices chosen
3 tbsp mayonnaise	from black mustard, celery seed,
3 tbsp plain yoghurt	cumin, fennel, fenugreek, nigella
1 tsp Dijon mustard	Salt and freshly ground black pepper

Prepare the celeriac as in the recipe above. For the dressing, mix together the mayonnaise, yoghurt, Dijon mustard, the juice of half a lemon, salt and pepper. Put a little olive oil in a frying pan and, when it is hot, add the spices. Allow them to pop and sizzle for a minute before adding to the mayonnaise dressing.

Drain the celeriac, pat dry with a tea towel and place in a bowl. Mix in the dressing and check seasoning.

CHICORY, ENDIVE, RADICCHIO AND TREVISO

Chicory in all its guises has been a bit player in our diet at least since Roman times and was much used in winter salads. Apicius has recipes we might use today; endives with brine, a little oil and chopped onions dressed with honey, and another for endive dressed with vinegar and honey. In England 'succory' was cultivated at least by the 16th century. By the 19th century chicory root was made into a substitute for coffee when trade or restrictions had stopped its import.

Nomenclature can be tricky. What in England is usually called chicory (a word which comes from the Persian) is the white or red tinged bud grown in the dark, mostly under the soil. I have not tried to grow it on the allotment. The green or curly endive is more dandelion-like. Other names for it are blue daisy, blue dandelion and wild bachelor's buttons. In southern England it still grows wild and has very attractive flowers.

Chicory, endive, radicchio and Treviso are all useful in winter salads. They do have a bitter taste and need careful dressing. Thyme is a complementary herb and a sweet dressing, with orange juice and soya sauce, can also work well. By cooking chicory the bitter taste is reduced.

On the allotment, by far the best crop to grow is radicchio. In salads, any of the chicory type vegetables are interchangeable.

RADICCHIO AND PRAWN SALAD

This recipe is inspired by Mark Hix who rightly believes there is something to be salvaged in this dish from the 1970s.

½ small cucumber
Cos lettuce
1 head endive
½ fennel, finely sliced (optional)
4 spring onions, trimmed and
　finely cut
400g prawns, cooked and peeled

For the dressing:
5 tbsp mayonnaise (see page 212)
4 tbsp tomato ketchup
2 tsp Worcestershire sauce
A few drops Tabasco
½ tbsp chopped dill
Salt and freshly ground black pepper
Wedges of lime to serve

Take slices of skin off the cucumber so it has a stripped appearance. Cut in half lengthways and scoop out the seeds. Slice finely. Shred the lettuce and endive. Place in a bowl together with the cucumber, fennel (if using), and spring onion.

Make the dressing by combining all the ingredients and seasoning with salt and pepper.

Arrange the salad on a plate (or in a glass to be truly retro), spoon on some of the mayonnaise dressing and put the prawns on top. Serve with a wedge of lime on the side of each plate.

CAULIFLOWER, RADICCHIO AND CAPER SALAD

Fine slices of raw cauliflower, mixed with finely prepared radicchio and a few capers served in a sauce made from twice the amount of olive oil to balsamic vinegar and seasoned with salt and freshly ground black pepper.

ROAST CHICORY TART

This is a savory version of Tarte Tatin.

2 chicory heads
1 carrot
1 turnip
1 large onion
1 bulb fennel
2 tbsp olive oil
Salt and freshly ground black pepper
1 red chilli, finely chopped
1 tsp thyme leaves
1 tbsp caster sugar
200g puff pastry bought or home-made

Prepare the vegetables and slice them, preferably with a mandoline. Spread them out on a baking sheet, pour over the oil and roast for about 10 minutes in a hot oven (200°C) until they are partially cooked and have some colour.

Melt the butter in a tarte tatin dish, sprinkle on the sugar, thyme leaves and chopped chilli. Arrange the seasoned vegetables on top.

Roll out the pastry and place it over the vegetables. Prick with a fork, then bake in the oven still set at 200°C for 20 minutes or so until the pastry is brown.

Leave to cool a little before turning onto a plate and serving.

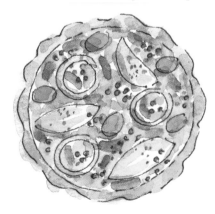

Grilled Radicchio or Treviso

4 heads of radicchio or Treviso
3 tbsp olive oil
Salt and freshly ground black pepper

Cut the prepared radicchio or Treviso into quarters lengthways and put on kitchen paper to remove any excess water. Place in a grill pan and sprinkle over the olive oil and season with salt and pepper.

Cook under the grill (or in a griddle pan if you prefer) for about 10 minutes, turning the quarters to ensure each side browns. Test by piercing the thickest part of the core to check it is cooked.

Transfer the radicchio or Treviso to a dish, spoon over any juices from the pan. Serve either tepid or cold. Radicchio grilled this way makes an excellent first course served with slivers of Gorgonzola.

Chicory Gratin

4 chicory heads, quartered lengthways
200g crème fraîche
1 tbsp Dijon mustard
1 tsp thyme leaves
200g white breadcrumbs
60g Parmesan cheese, finely grated
75g butter

Fit the chicory quarters into an oven proof dish. In a small saucepan, simmer the crème fraîche, mustard and thyme leaves for a few minutes until slightly reduced. Season and pour over the chicory. Scatter the breadcrumbs and cheese over the chicory. Melt the butter and pour over the top.

Roast at 180°C for about 40 minutes or until chicory is cooked and the top is brown.

COURGETTES AND MARROW

In most summers, courgettes are the bounty crop. All members of the squash family have their origins in North America. An Iroquois myth tells the story of three inseparable sisters, symbolized as corn, beans and squashes. As the names of some popular varieties testify, courgettes, or zucchini, were developed in Italy in the 19th century. It wasn't until the 1970s that they became popular in England. It was only in 1980 that Marshalls introduced courgette seeds to their catalogue.

Slugs and snails attack courgettes and mildew can be a problem but, when the crop is heavy, it is a luxury to use the flowers and infant fruit. Overgrown courgettes have their uses too. They can be cut into rings and roasted, stuffed with a meat or lentil sauce.

Courgette Soup

Variations on courgette soup are endless. As well as courgettes, most recipes include chicken stock, onion, and butter. There are even recipes for soup using marrow flowers. Herbs give variety and the addition of potato or watercress makes for a thicker soup. Grated Parmesan cheese is always a welcome accompaniment.

Soupe Menerboise, almost a French version of minestrone, where the courgettes, finely cubed, are cooked with onions, tomatoes, broad beans, pasta and, at the end, egg yolks, served with Parmesan cheese, is a lovely soup for late summer.

Courgette Flower Tempura

These are fun to make and always impressive. Slivers of quick melting cheese can be inserted inside the flowers.

12 courgette flowers
Vegetable oil

For the batter:

200ml iced water
75g plain flour
1tsp baking powder
25g potato flour
Salt and freshly ground black pepper

Make the batter by gradually mixing the iced water into the two flours, baking powder and seasoning.

Wash the courgette flowers.

Preheat the vegetable oil. Dip the flowers in the batter and drop them into the fat for a few minutes until crisp. Remove with a slotted spoon and dry on kitchen paper.

Serve immediately.

Marrow Salad

This salad is an annual treat. A small marrow is ideal for this dish but not if the skin is tough. Kitchen paper plays a vital part in nearly every stage. The cook does need to be vigilant and the salad should be served as soon as the slices are cool otherwise their crispness is lost.

1 small marrow
Plain flour
Salt
Olive oil
Juice of one lemon
Chopped parsley

Cut off the ends of the marrow and slice in two lengthwise. Scoop out seeds and, using a mandoline, slice the marrow into very thin semicircular slices. Salt for ½ hour or more in a colander to remove excess liquid. Rinse and pat dry.

In a deep sided frying pan or wok heat some olive oil. Lightly flour the courgette slices and fry them in the oil in batches, turning over the slices so that they brown on each side. Do not try to cook too many at a time as they will not cook crisply. If the olive oil becomes too floury, wipe the frying pan or wok clean with kitchen paper and start again using fresh oil. As the slices cook, drain them on kitchen paper before putting them in a dish and adding lemon juice.

Serve decorated with chopped parsley.

Courgette and Goat's Cheese Soufflé

2 courgettes
60g butter plus extra for greasing
30g plain flour
290ml milk
100g crumbly goat's cheese
4 eggs, separated
Salt and freshly ground black pepper
Grated Parmesan cheese

Lightly butter a soufflé dish.

Grate the courgettes and place in a colander. Sprinkle on salt and leave for 30 minutes to remove excess liquid. Rinse and pat dry. Fry them gently in half of the butter until soft but not coloured.

Melt the remaining butter in a small saucepan. Remove from the heat and stir in the flour with a wooden spoon. Return to the heat and cook gently until the mixture bubbles. Gradually stir in the milk to make a smooth sauce. Then, stirring constantly, allow the sauce to boil for a minute or two. Remove from the heat and stir in the egg yolks, crumbled cheese and the courgettes.

Whisk the egg whites until they are just stiff. Mix a spoonful of the egg whites into the soufflé mixture to loosen it and then, using a large metal spoon, fold in the remaining whites.

Pour the mixture into the prepared dish and sprinkle over the top a little grated Parmesan cheese. Place the dish in a roasting pan and add enough water to the pan for the dish to stand in a few centimetres of water.

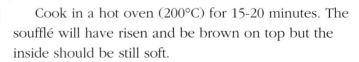

Cook in a hot oven (200°C) for 15-20 minutes. The soufflé will have risen and be brown on top but the inside should be still soft.

Roast Chicken Stuffed with Courgettes under the Skin

I keep the now faded *Sunday Times* article from the 1970s in which Richard Olney was visited in the South of France and prepared this dish. It was very obvious that he was an exquisite cook. In his version, the chicken is spatchcocked.

A medium free range chicken	2 eggs
3 courgettes	Small tub of Ricotta
Salt	Generous serving of Parmesan
125g butter	Salt and freshly ground black pepper

First, prepare the chicken. Using your fingers and a wooden spoon, carefully separate the skin from the breast of the chicken. Work around, going down the sides, taking care not to split the skin at the neck. If the skin does break, do not worry as it can always be sewn up before cooking.

Finely grate the courgettes and put them in a colander with salt so that the juices are extracted. Leave for at least ½ hour and then rinse. Using your hands, squeeze out as much of the remaining water as possible.

Melt the butter in a heavy-bottomed frying pan and add the courgettes. Cook gently until the courgettes are soft but not coloured. Put to one side to cool.

Whisk the eggs with the cheeses and a generous seasoning of pepper and add to the courgettes.

Carefully fill the chicken by introducing the stuffing, a large spoon at a time, working it in to cover the breast. Sew up the skin if it has broken around the neck. Sprinkle a little salt over the chicken.

Put the chicken in a roasting pan and cook at 190°C for ½ hour and then turn down the heat to 170°C for a further hour or until the chicken is thoroughly cooked. Towards the end of roasting, the skin and any escaped stuffing will start to blacken. A sheet of aluminum foil over the breast will protect it.

When cooked, leave the chicken to rest for five minutes before carving.

Courgette and Feta Fritters

3 courgettes
2 shallots, finely chopped
2 cloves garlic, crushed
60g self-raising flour
2 eggs
1 tsp ground coriander
½ tsp ground cardamom
Zest of 1 lime
150g Feta cheese
Sunflower oil
Salt and freshly ground black pepper

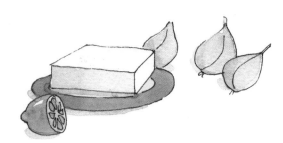

Grate the courgettes and put them in a colander with salt and leave for half an hour. Squeeze the courgettes to remove excess liquid.

Put the courgettes in a bowl with the shallots, garlic, flour, eggs, spices, and lime zest. Mix the ingredients to form a thick batter, season and then add the Feta cheese, crumbled.

Heat the oil in a large frying pan and, using a soup spoon to form the fritters, fry them in batches. Cook them for approximately three minutes on each side and flatten them out slightly while cooking.

Drain on kitchen paper and serve with sour cream to which chopped coriander and lime juice have been added.

CUCUMBER

The Emperor Tiberius was an early fan of cucumber which, to support his request for it to be offered daily at his table, was grown in specially constructed miniature glass houses on wheels that could be rolled to the best position to find winter sun. Charlemagne too grew cucumbers in his garden but perhaps what both emperors grew was more like a gherkin than the cucumber we know today.

Cucumbers were grown in England by the fourteenth century but were not widely grown until hot houses became fashionable in Edwardian England and cucumbers with their tendrils provided decorative cover. Early cookery books mostly give unappetizing recipes for cooking cucumbers. Home grown cucumbers have so much more taste.

*"A cucumber should be
well sliced and dressed with pepper
and vinegar, and then thrown out, as
good for nothing."*

Samuel Johnson, quoted in Boswell's
*Journal of a Tour to the Hebrides
with Samuel Johnson,*
Oct 5, 1773

TARATOR

A delicious Bulgarian summer soup, best served very cold and quite thin.

1 litre plain yoghurt
1 litre ice-cold water
2 cucumbers, peeled and chopped into soup-sized pieces
1 small handful mint, finely chopped
1 small handful flat-leaf parsley, finely chopped
1 medium handful dill, finely chopped
2 tbsp olive oil
4–5 cloves garlic, crushed
Salt and freshly ground black pepper

Holding back some of the water, stir all the ingredients together, adding more water until the required consistency is reached. Season to taste. Serve very cold with good crusty bread.

CUCUMBER SANDWICHES

A delicacy of great simplicity, redolent of tea parties and immortalized by Lady Bracknell.

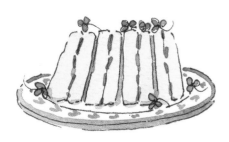

It is crucial that all the elements are of the best quality. Peel the cucumber in stripes so that a hint of the green skin remains. Slice very thinly. Place on the freshest white buttered bread and sprinkle with salt and freshly ground white pepper. Make up into sandwiches and serve with the crusts removed.

CUCUMBER SALAD

This is so good that Connie Garforth makes it, by universal request, for every French class party. The recipe is based on one of Yotam Ottolenghi's.

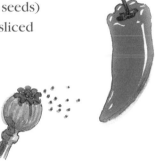

2-3 cucumbers (choose slim ones with small seeds)
1 mild red chilli pepper, deseeded and thinly sliced
3 tbsp chopped fresh coriander leaves
4 tbsp white wine vinegar
5 tbsp sunflower oil
2 tbsp poppy seeds
2 tbsp caster sugar
 Salt and freshly ground black pepper

Wash the cucumbers and cut off the ends. Halve them lengthwise and then cut the halved sections at an angle, into long, very fine slices. Ignoring the first slices which will be mostly skin, put the rest into a large bowl. Add coriander leaves, vinegar, oil, chilli, poppy seeds and sugar, then season with salt and pepper. Infuse the flavours by moving the cucumber around in the bowl. Serve immediately.

EXPERIMENTING WITH CUCUMBER

The essence of a cucumber salad is that it should be refreshing. Cucumber gives the opportunity to create new salads in which acidity is balanced by sweetness. Dill, mint or chives with yoghurt and salt make a good salad to go with Mediterranean dishes. Borage flowers give colour and intensity. Pounded garlic and ginger with sesame oil, toasted sesame seeds, and vinegar give an oriental flavour. Red onions and fennel give sweetness. I especially like red onions and red chillies very finely chopped, served on sliced cucumber that has been lightly dressed.

PICKLED CUCUMBERS WITH GARLIC AND MUSTARD SEEDS

A light pickle for use within two months.

6 small or 3 large cucumbers
2 tbsp salt
500ml white wine vinegar
3 tbsp caster sugar
2 tsp yellow mustard seeds
1 tsp poppy seeds
5 garlic cloves, thinly sliced

Preferably using a mandoline, cut the cucumbers into thin, oblique slices. Put them into a large bowl, sprinkling salt between each layer. Cover and leave to stand overnight.

Put the vinegar and remaining ingredients into a pan and heat carefully until the sugar is dissolved. Do not let it boil. Allow to cool.

Using sterilized kilner jars, loosely pack in the cucumbers and fill up the jars with the vinegar solution and seal. Once jars are opened, store them in the fridge and use within 10 days.

CURRANTS — BLACK, RED, AND WHITE

Both black- and redcurrants have intense flavours. In years when the crop is small, a few currants of either variety can be used to give taste to a creamy dessert. White currants, an albino variant of redcurrant, have a sweeter but blander taste. They make a wonderful dessert jelly.

Most of the commercial production of blackcurrants in England is used to make blackcurrant cordial but small producers, such as Jo Hilditch in Herefordshire, are making excellent cassis, the blackcurrant liqueur.

Redcurrants have a much sharper taste. Redcurrant jelly is traditionally served with roast lamb or venison. Bar-le-Duc has been the centre of currant jam production in France since the fourteenth century. Exquisite jams are made from red and white currants that have been deseeded using a goose quill. The jam was said to have been a favourite of Mary Queen of Scots. Today only one confiturière remains, Anne Dutriez, who has taken over from her grandfather to keep the tradition alive.

In northern and eastern Europe there is a stronger tradition of using redcurrants in puddings. One dessert, a semolina pudding made with redcurrant juice whisked into a mousse and floated on milk, called variants of Pink Manna or Manna from Heaven, is comfort food from Estonia to Bulgaria. Flummery in the raspberry chapter uses much the same ingredients.

Chopped fresh or dried, the leaves of blackcurrants can be made into a tisane by adding boiled water. It is good drink for the dark days of winter.

I learnt to my cost that black- and redcurrant bushes should be pruned differently. The blackcurrant fruits on older wood which can be cut back after harvesting while redcurrants need the shoots from the main branches to be cut into long spurs. Luckily currant bushes are very forgiving and a severe pruning can, ultimately, be beneficial.

BLACKCURRANT COULIS

A coulis made with freshly picked fruit has a myriad of uses. With vanilla ice cream (see page 220), a pannacotta (see pages 216-17), rice pudding (see page 215), pancakes or waffles (see page 219), or made into a mousse. Coulis freezes well and can be very useful when impromptu entertaining calls for a speedy dessert. As Nigel Slater notes, a pastry or crumble crust will 'do nothing' for red or white currants but blackcurrants do mix well with oats and can be used to make a variant of cranachan.

250g blackcurrants or blackcurrants and raspberries,
50g caster sugar

There is no need to take off the stalks but wash the fruit and cook slowly in a pan (with the raspberries, if using) until the fruit is soft. Add sugar, stir until dissolved, and then remove from the heat and sieve. Serve either hot or cold.

BLACKCURRANT JAM

Glistening blackcurrant jam is a special tea time treat.

1.75 kg blackcurrants
1 litre water
2.20 kg granulated sugar

Rinse the blackcurrants and strip them from the stalks. Put them in a preserving pan with the water and simmer gently until the fruit is soft. Stir occasionally to be sure the fruit is not sticking.

Add the sugar, warmed, and stir until it is dissolved. Increase the heat and boil for about 15-20 minutes until the jam is set.

REDCURRANT MAZARIN TART

300g sweet crust pastry (see page 214)

200g ground almonds

200g golden caster sugar

100g butter, softened

100g cornflour

2 tsp vanilla essence

4 eggs

300g redcurrants, washed and destalked

Bring the pastry from the fridge and roll it out to fit a 23cm pie dish. Lift it into the dish and gently press it to the sides. Trim away any excess pastry. Prick the base of the pastry with a fork, line with baking paper and, using baking beans, bake blind in an oven heated to 190°C for 20 minutes or until the pastry begins to brown.

While the pastry is baking, combine ground almonds, sugar, butter, cornflour, vanilla essence and eggs (you can do this in a blender or food processor). Pour onto the pastry, smooth over with a knife, and place the redcurrants on top.

Return to the oven and cook for about 20 minutes until the tart is golden and well risen.

Vanilla Bean Brulée with Blackcurrants

500 ml double cream
2 vanilla pods
7 egg yolks
110g caster sugar
225g blackcurrants
25g caster sugar for caramelising

Place the cream in a heavy-based pan. Slit the vanilla pods lengthwise and scrape the seeds into the cream. Bring almost to the boil, being careful that the cream doesn't brown on the base of the pan, and leave aside for 30 minutes.

Whisk the egg yolks and sugar together until pale and fluffy. Strain the cream and vanilla onto the eggs and whisk together. Put the blackcurrants in the bottom of six ramekins and pour custard on top. Place on a baking tray with water an inch deep (or use a bain marie) and bake at 170°C for 30 minutes until firm to the touch. Leave to cool and then sprinkle with sugar and caramelize under the grill.

Raspberries can be used in the same way.

Redcurrant, White Currant and Cherry Fool

This quick and easy mousse makes the most of summer fruit. Use whatever fruits are in season, varying the amount of sugar accordingly.

250g redcurrants, plus 4 sprigs to garnish
250g white currants
250g ripe black cherries, pitted
4 tbsp icing sugar
200 ml double cream
Seeds from 1 vanilla pod
200 ml Greek yoghurt

Wash and strip redcurrants and white currants from their stalks. Cut the cherries into quarters. Place two-thirds of the fruit and two tablespoons of the sugar into a blender or food processor and blend to a purée. Then push the mixture through a sieve to remove the seeds.

Whisk the double cream, vanilla seeds and remaining sugar until stiff. Fold in the yoghurt, followed by the fruit purée. Finally, stir through the remaining fruit, being careful not to mix it in too well and so losing a ripple effect.

Spoon the mousse into 4 chilled glasses and garnish each with a spray of redcurrants. Chill until ready to serve.

REDCURRANT JELLY

Our redcurrants ripen in the second half of July and need to be carefully watched. Birds can swoop and destroy the crop in a day. Netting helps but can create the added problem of birds becoming trapped. Redcurrant jelly is perfect with roast lamb or game.

Imperial measurements come into their own in jam making; a pint of liquid to a pound (lb) of sugar.

A bucket full of redcurrants
Granulated sugar

Wash the redcurrants, leaving on their stalks. Put them in a preserving pan and add water. How much water very much depends on the ripeness of the fruit but, as a general rule, add enough water to almost cover the fruit. Use less water if the fruit is very ripe. Cook gently until the fruit is soft. Allow to cool and then strain through a muslin cloth or jelly bag.

Measure the juice and allow 450g sugar to every 550 ml of juice. Heat juice and sugar together in a preserving pan, stirring until the sugar has dissolved. Then boil, removing scum from time to time, until a good set is achieved. This should not take long.

Although this jelly keeps well, once opened, any jar should be stored in the fridge.

FENNEL

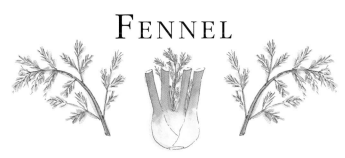

Mark Hix's Galette au Fenouil from The Ivy is a revelation. I had not thought of using fennel in a dessert. Raw fennel makes very refreshing salads. Its aniseed taste goes especially well with smoked fish or pork. On my allotment, fennel, both bronze and normal, grows every year. I keep it to use the fern (leaves), which look like but do not taste the same as dill, and for the buds and seeds. The true vegetable is Florentine fennel which produces the bulb and it is these seeds that are sold commercially. The Greek for wild fennel is 'marathon' and the famous Greek battle site was on a field of fennel.

In March 2012, Elizabeth Gunnison wrote an article about fennel in the *Wall Street Journal*. She called the fennel buds 'Culinary Fairy Dust'. In fact they were already known in the US as 'fennel pollen'. Indeed, there is some magic in fennel buds. They can augment and transform the taste of breads or risotto and are delicious in a ravioli with Ricotta and crème fraîche. Buds or seeds rubbed on pork or veal intensify the flavour.

SALAD OF FENNEL, CUCUMBER AND RADISH

Cut an unpeeled cucumber into slices the width of a pound coin and then cut the slices into quarters. Slice a fennel bulb into parchment-thick strips and cut up some radishes. Mix together and dress with chopped mint, salt, freshly ground black pepper, garlic, olive oil and lemon juice.

SALAD OF FENNEL AND ORANGE

Two oranges, either blood or navel, that have been carefully peeled and thinly sliced make a wonderful salad with the thinnest slivers of fennel and red onion, served on a bed of watercress and dressed with the following:

2 tbsp olive oil
1 tbsp light soya sauce
1 tbsp orange juice
Salt and freshly ground black pepper

Pomegranate seeds could be used to decorate.

MARINATED FENNEL

This way of preparing fennel is delicious with fish.

Reserve any fennel ferns and then slice the fennel finely, preferably with a mandoline. Chop the ferns and mix with a tablespoon of crushed fennel seeds, or seeds and buds, salt, freshly ground black pepper, a little sugar, and equal quantities of white wine vinegar and olive oil. Mix well and pour over the fennel.

Leave for an hour before serving.

COD WITH FENNEL, LEEKS AND TOMATOES

A popular meal for Friday evenings. The vegetables can be cooked in advance.

500g cod or other white fish
250g tomatoes, skinned, seeded, and chopped
350g leeks, cleaned, trimmed, and finely chopped
350g fennel bulb, finely sliced
Small bunch salad onions, cleaned and sliced at an angle
Olive oil

Pour a generous amount of olive oil into a sauté pan and carefully cook the fennel, leeks, and spring onions. They are expected to colour. When the vegetables begin to soften, add the tomatoes and season. Leave to cook for about 15 minutes or until the sauce is thick.

Spread the mixture onto a baking dish, place the fish fillets on top and sprinkle over more olive oil. Bake at 190°C for 15 minutes or until the fish is cooked. Serve immediately.

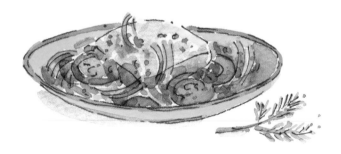

Mark Hix's Galette au Fenouil

200g puff pastry (bought or home-made)
1kg fennel
300g caster sugar
2 tsp fennel seeds
Icing sugar for dusting
200g crème fraîche

Trim the fennel bulbs, keeping to one side any ferns. Put the whole fennel into a saucepan with the sugar and fennel seeds. Cover with water, bring to the boil and simmer gently for one hour until the fennel is soft to the point of a knife.

Roll out the pastry and make four discs, 12cm diameter, in the pastry, using a saucepan lid or plate as a template. Prick over with a fork then leave to rest for an hour in the fridge.

Put the discs on a baking tray and cover with a wire rack to stop them rising. Bake at 200°C for seven minutes then take out of the oven, remove the rack, turn over the pastry before returning to the rack and cooking for a further four minutes. Take them out and put to one side.

Strain half of the cooking syrup through a fine-meshed sieve into a clean pan and simmer until it is reduced to about 4 or 5 tablespoons. Remove from heat, leave to cool, then add the fennel fern, finely chopped.

Cut the fennel bulbs lengthways into ½cm slices and arrange on the pastry discs in a circles, going to the very edges of the discs. Dust with icing sugar and bake for a further 7-8 minutes. Serve with crème fraîche and the syrup spooned around.

GARLIC

G arlic comes in two versions, the bulbs and the wild garlic to be picked in shady places for much of the spring. Around Bath, the smell gives away the best locations. Both are alliums though not closely related. They taste similar and in many recipes are interchangeable. The flavour of wild garlic is less pungent. It is mostly used for its leaves. Both types have pretty flowers which can be used to decorate salads.

Garlic bulbs are planted in the early autumn. It is surprisingly easy to grow and very useful to have on hand. Take care not to use garlic which is old and stale.

Aïoli is the classic garlic sauce. This can either be made by crushing two cloves into the bowl before adding the egg yolks to make mayonnaise or by adding a teaspoon or two of puréed wild garlic leaves into the mayonnaise before serving.

Linguine with Garlic and Chilli

The simplest and best of all pasta sauces is simply garlic, olive oil and chilli flakes. While the pasta is cooking, put the crushed garlic in heated oil for a few moments with some chilli flakes. Do not let the garlic colour. Take off the heat and stir into the pasta, which Italians will confirm should be barely drained and still dripping wet. Serve with Parmesan cheese.

If such simplicity seems alien, pancetta, cut into 1 cm cubes could be fried with the garlic, or anchovies and chopped parsley could be added to the sauce.

Hummus

150g chickpeas
Salt
4 garlic cloves
Juice of 1 lemon
3 tbsp olive oil
2 tbsp light tahini paste
Paprika

Soak the chickpeas in water over night. Drain them and put them in a large saucepan and cover with fresh water. Bring to the boil and then let simmer for 2-4 hours or until the chickpeas are tender. Season with salt at the end of cooking.

Drain the chickpeas, reserving some of the cooking liquid.

Peel the garlic and put into a blender with the chickpeas, tahini paste, lemon juice, two tablespoons of olive oil and blend, using enough of the cooking liquid as necessary to make a thick paste.

Put into a dish, sprinkle over a little paprika and the rest of the olive oil. Serve with pitta bread. Together with olives, some pickled vegetables and rustic cheese, this makes a perfect lunch.

If time is short, two tins of chickpeas could be substituted for the dried ones.

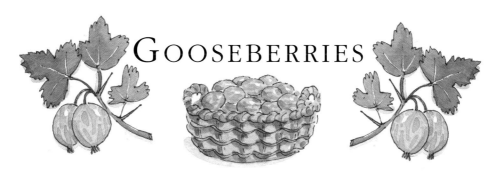

GOOSEBERRIES

Gooseberries are the fruit of NW Europe. In 1275 gooseberries are mentioned having been ordered for planting in the garden of the Tower of London. Norwegians call them *stikkelsbæ* (prickly berry) and in Holland, where they were first cultivated, they are known as kruisberie. In France there is no great tradition of cooking gooseberries beyond the sauce for serving with mackerel, as their name, *groseille à maquereaux*, implies.

Charles Darwin grew 54 varieties of gooseberries in the garden of his home at Down House, Kent and used them in research for his book, *Variations of Animals and Plants under Domestication*, 1868. These days only about 10 varieties are sold commercially of which Careless and Invicta are the best known. The large, pink, dessert varieties do not cook well.

Even Darwin didn't manage to divest gooseberries of the hairs on the fruit or sharp spikes on the branches. Picking and pruning are jobs needing strong gloves and long sleeves.

Elderflowers are the ideal flavour for gooseberries and could be used in any of the desserts. Add the stems of elderflowers while cooking the gooseberries but extract them when the gooseberries have cooled. I am also very fond of ginger with gooseberries.

Gooseberry Sauce for Mackerel
(or Sorrel Sauce for Veal)

Elizabeth David in *French Provincial Cooking* devotes a whole chapter to sauces. She remarks, surprisingly, that Purée D'Oseille (Sorrel sauce) is almost indistinguishable from gooseberry sauce. Jane Grigson gives three different recipes for gooseberry sauce, including Elizabeth David's, in her book, *Fish Cooking*. As both writers agree, by substituting a handful of sorrel leaves for the gooseberries, this becomes Sorrel sauce, delicious served with veal or poached eggs.

20g butter
300g gooseberries
75 ml double cream or
50 ml cream and 25 ml milk

Stock or juice from cooking
  the fish (or veal)
Salt
Freshly ground black pepper

Top and tail the gooseberries, cook them on a low heat with the butter until just soft. Allow to cool, and then sieve them.

Put the cream in a milk pan and bring to the boil. Add a tablespoon or two of stock and add to the gooseberry purée. Season. If the gooseberries are very tart, you may want to add a teaspoon of sugar. Serve warm.

Gooseberry Jam

The hard part is picking and then topping and tailing the fruit, as this is a very easy jam to make. Neither lemon nor pectin is needed. The jam is better made with unripe fruit.

3 kg gooseberries
3.5 kg granulated sugar
300 ml water

Top and tail, then wash the gooseberries. Put them in the preserving pan with the water and simmer for about 20 minutes until opaque and soft. If the fruit starts to stick to the bottom of the pan, tip the contents into a large bowl, wash out the preserving pan before returning the fruit to the pan and continuing to cook. Add the sugar, warmed, and stir over a gentle heat until it has dissolved, then boil rapidly for 15-20 minutes, removing the scum from time to time, until the jam is set when tested. When ready, pour into clean, warmed jars. Towards the end of cooking, the jam will magically transform to a wonderful pink colour.

Gooseberry Fool

'Nursery food' which I loved as a child and still love. It is best to use slightly under ripe fruit for this dish.

900g gooseberries
225g sugar
300 ml double cream

Wash the gooseberries (no need to top and tail them) and steam them until they are soft. Mix in the sugar, allow to cool and then sieve them. Whisk the cream until thick and stir into the gooseberry purée. Pour into individual bowls and keep cool before serving.

GOOSEBERRY ICE CREAM

900g gooseberries
175g caster sugar
400 ml double cream

Zested peel of 1 orange
3 tbsp water

Place the gooseberries, sugar, and zested orange peel in a saucepan with the water. Cover and cook on a low heat until the gooseberries are soft. Rub through a sieve and leave to cool. Lightly whip the cream until it begins to thicken, stir into the gooseberry purée and pour into the ice cream maker. Store in the deep freeze but put into the fridge 30 minutes before use. Serve with a brandy snap.

BRANDY SNAPS

Ginger goes well with gooseberries. Make snaps to fill with gooseberry fool or form trefoil baskets for ice cream.

40g golden syrup
40g butter
80g caster sugar
40g plain flour

Scant tsp ground ginger
Scant tsp finely grated orange
 rind
A few drops orange juice

Gently heat the syrup, butter, and sugar together, stirring occasionally until the sugar has dissolved. Remove from the heat and stir in the other ingredients.

To make snaps, drop teaspoons of the mixture, spaced well apart, onto greased baking trays. Cook at 160°C for about eight minutes or until the mixture is spread around and rich brown in colour.

Leave on the tray for a few minutes to firm. Then, using a fish slice, lift them off the tray and, with the underneath to the outside, form the snaps by shaping them around the handle of a wooden spoon. Leave to set on a wire rack.

HEDGEROW FRUITS

Most of my hedgerow harvest is from the edges of the fields outside Wells where our horses are kept. First to pick are elderflowers, then apples, perhaps the relic of a Somerset orchard. They are followed by brambles, elderberries, wild plums, crabapples, damsons, and, finally, sloes. There are walnuts, cobnuts, figs, quinces and medlars on the allotment site. Alas, the two cherry trees have gone. The hedgerows give relief from all the hard work on an allotment. Brambling on a perfect day in early September is one of my favourite moments of the year.

ELDERFLOWER CORDIAL

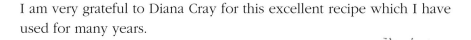

I am very grateful to Diana Cray for this excellent recipe which I have used for many years.

25 heads of elderflower
1.5kg granulated sugar
1.2 litres water
4 lemons
50g citric acid

Collect large clusters of white elderflowers on a sunny day when there has been no rain for at least two days previously. The smell of the elderflowers gives a clue to the right day. Do not wash the elderflowers but shake them well to remove any 'foreign bodies' and place in a large bowl.

Put the sugar in a pan with the water and slowly bring to the boil until the sugar dissolves. Remove from the heat and allow to cool before adding the zest of two of the lemons (taken off with a potato peeler). Slice all four lemons and add to the bowl with the elderflowers. Pour over the sugar syrup and add the citric acid. Leave for 48 hours.

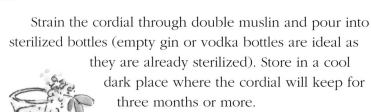

Strain the cordial through double muslin and pour into sterilized bottles (empty gin or vodka bottles are ideal as they are already sterilized). Store in a cool dark place where the cordial will keep for three months or more.

ELDERFLOWER FRITTERS

12 freshly picked elderflower heads with stalks
2 egg whites
250g cornflour
25g icing sugar, sifted
250 ml carbonated water
Sunflower oil for deep frying
Icing sugar

Shake each elderflower head to remove any insects. Sift the cornflour and sugar into a bowl. Add the egg whites and, by degrees, enough of the carbonated water to make a batter the consistency of single cream.

Heat sunflower oil approximately 2cm depth in a pan or wok, until it sizzles. Hold the elderflower head by the stalk. Dip it into the batter and then gently place it into the hot oil and fry until lightly golden.

Remove from the pan, dust with icing sugar. Serve immediately, with crème fraîche.

ELDERBERRY DRESSING FOR GAME

Elderberries go wonderfully with game. It is worth picking extra berries to store in the deep freeze during the game season just to add to casseroles and sauces.

2 tbsp red wine vinegar
4 tbsp olive oil
50g elderberries
Salt and freshly ground black pepper

Pick the elderberries from their stalks. Mix the vinegar and oil together, season and add the elderberries. Allow to infuse for an hour or so before using.

SUMMER PUDDING

As simple as this recipe may sound, it takes time (two nights and one day) to make.

800g summer fruits.
  These can be blackcurrants, raspberries,
  redcurrants, loganberries, tayberries, or later
  in the season, elderberries or, blackberries
  (so evolving into Autumn Pudding). Do not
  use strawberries, which do not have the
  right texture.
150g caster sugar or more, depending on the
  sweetness of the fruit
6 or more thin slices of day old white bread,
  crusts removed

Put the fruit and sugar into a bowl and leave overnight. The next day tip the contents into a pan, bring to the boil and gently simmer for a very few minutes until the fruit is lightly cooked. Allow to cool. Line a basin with cling film, then line with the slices of bread, making a round piece to fit the bottom and overlapping the side pieces so there are no gaps.

Spoon the fruit and most of the juice into a basin until it is almost full. Place one more round piece of bread to fit the top, trimming the sides so that it fits neatly. Put a plate on top of the bowl with some weights so that the pudding is pressed down and all the bread is infused with the fruit juice. Leave in the fridge overnight.

To serve, place a serving dish on top and invert the basin so that the pudding falls free onto the plate.

Serve with lashings of thick cream and the remaining reserved juice in a jug.

DAMSON CHUTNEY

❖

Set aside a day to make this chutney.

2kg damsons

500g cooking apples, cored and
  chopped

3 onions, peeled and chopped,

3 cloves garlic, skinned and finely
  chopped

500g raisins

3 tsp ground ginger

1 tbsp allspice berries

1 tbsp cloves

1 star anise

2 sticks cinnamon

500g dark soft brown sugar

500g demerara sugar

2 tbsp salt

1.75 litres malt vinegar

To get things started, and to avoid having to use spice bags, I like
to put the whole allspice, star anise, cloves and cinnamon sticks in
a saucepan with about 400 ml of the vinegar, bring to the boil, then
allow to barely simmer for half an hour. Put to one side to cool.

Wash the damsons and put them in a saucepan. Cover them with
more of the vinegar. Simmer until the damsons are soft. Allow to cool
a little before taking out the stones. This can be a messy business but
many of the stones will have risen to the top and can be removed with
a perforated spoon. A final check can be made by wearing rubber
gloves and feeling around in the flesh for any that remain hidden.

Put the damson flesh, prepared apples, onions, garlic, raisins,
sugars, ground ginger, salt, and remaining vinegar into a preserving
pan. Add to this the vinegar strained from the spices.

Cook slowly for 2-3 hours, stirring occasionally checking that the
chutney is not sticking to the bottom of the pan.

When the chutney is thick and not watery (pass a
wooden spoon through the middle of the chutney to
check), pack into prepared jars and seal.

Store for at least a month before using.

QUINCE CHEESE

1kg quinces
800g sugar
Juice of 3 lemons

Wash the quinces and, without peeling or coring, cut them into chunks. Put them into a saucepan and cover with water. Simmer for 30 minutes or more until the quinces are soft.

Mash the fruit and then rub it through a sieve. Put the purée in the preserving pan, add the sugar and lemon juice and, stirring frequently, simmer until the sugar has dissolved.

Then increase the heat and cook, stirring vigilantly, until the cheese is thick. If it does start to stick to the bottom of the pan in the final stages of cooking, remove the cheese mixture to a clean bowl, wash and dry the preserving pan thoroughly before returning the contents and continuing to cook.

Test by pushing a wooden spoon across the cheese to see if it leaves a clear separation and when ready, store in shallow, straight-sided freezer containers with lids, that have been lined with greaseproof paper or brushed with a little glycerine.

AUTUMN FRUIT COULIS

Damsons, blackberries, even elderberries, gently stewed with sugar, then either blended or left whole make a wonderful sauce to go with ice creams, pancakes, cereals or cheesecake.

I freeze these in small bags for use all through winter. Coulis blended further with a banana and plain yoghurt makes a perfect 'smoothie', ideal for breakfast.

DAMSON SORBET

900g damsons
275g caster sugar

Stew the fruit with sugar in very little water until soft.
Sieve the pulp. Allow to cool and make sorbet in an
ice cream maker.

MEDLAR JELLY

2kg medlars
1kg sugar (approx.)
Juice of 3 lemons

The beginning of this jelly is the most exciting part, as the medlars
are left to blet. For this recipe use medlars that are soft but not
over-bletted.

Wash the medlars and cut in half. Put in a preserving pan with
enough water to barely cover and simmer gently for 30 minutes or
more until the fruit is soft and mushy.

Strain the pulp through muslin overnight and then measure the
liquid. Put the liquid in the preserving pan with the lemon juice, heat
slowly and add warmed sugar. For every 500ml of liquid
you will need 400g of sugar.

Let the jelly boil actively until it is set and
store in warmed, prepared jars.

Blackberry and Apple Jelly

I love this jelly for its taste of autumn and the day spent gathering blackberries. It is important to choose the right day when the blackberries are warm from the sun and not still wet with rain. I pick in the fields where our horses are kept. They are very inquisitive.

2kg blackberries
1kg wild or cooking apples
Sugar

Wash the fruit and cut the apples into pieces without peeling or coring them. Put the fruit into a pan with about a pint of water. Simmer gently for an hour or until very soft. Cool.

Tie the pulp into a jelly bag and leave to drip overnight. Measure the juice and pour into a preserving pan. Add 400g sugar for every 500 ml of juice. Place over a medium heat and stir until sugar dissolves. Bring to the boil and boil for 10 minutes and then test for setting.

When ready, pour into warmed, clean jars and seal.

Sloe Gin

Richard Mabey rightly calls this the most agreeable of liqueurs. Sloes are the ancestor of all cultivated plums. Excavations on a Neolithic site at Glastonbury uncovered a cash of sloe stones stored in a straw lined pit, evidence of an ancient process, known across Europe, by which sloes were rendered sweeter.

Pick sloes after the first frost or certainly in October after the weather has turned. Pierce each sloe (unless a hard frost has softened the skin) and half fill an empty gin bottle. Add half the weight of the sloes with sugar and fill the bottle with gin. Seal tightly and store in a cool place. Shake from time to time. The gin will turn vibrant pink.

The liquid can be decanted and should be ready to drink by Christmas but we prefer to leave the bottles for at least a year.

Walnut Leaf Liqueur

I must thank David Kelland for this recipe which puts empty vodka bottles to good use.

100 young walnut leaves
500 ml or more vodka
1 bottle red wine

1 bottle sweet white wine, such
as Sauternes
500g sugar

Towards the end of June, pick 100 very young and tender walnut leaves. Pack them into an empty vodka bottle. Fill up with vodka, seal tightly, and leave in a cool place for three months.

Strain the liquid through a fine mesh into a bowl. Add the sugar, then enough, equally, of white wine and red wine to produce the right amount of liquid to fill two empty vodka bottles.

When the sugar has dissolved, fill the bottles, seal them, and keep for three months or more before using which, conveniently, should be Christmas.

Spiced Roasted Walnuts

These are easily made and delicious to serve with drinks.

400g walnut halves
½ jar clear honey
200 ml water

1 tbsp walnut oil
1 tbsp salt
1 tsp cayenne pepper

Put the honey and water in a large saucepan with the walnuts and slowly bring to the boil. Cook gently for 10 minutes. Drain the walnuts and dry them on kitchen towels. Place on a roasting tray with oil and mix in the cayenne pepper. Roast the walnuts for about 10-15 minutes at 180°C, checking and moving them around the tray during the last minutes of cooking to be sure they brown evenly to a rich caramel colour. Salt them while still hot, then spread them out to cool on a rack.

When cold, store in an airtight container.

CARAMEL FIGS

Figs have a history in my family. Great Uncle Arthur, living in Shoreham-by-Sea, had the most prolific fig tree in his garden. Every summer he would send us packages of figs. I wish cuttings had been taken from that tree.

I would like to have had a whole chapter on figs but concede they are not typical allotment fruit. Ours grow against old walls on the edge of the allotment site. Years and crops vary. Last year our young tree had only two figs, but both weighed over 200g and were delicious. We ate them raw, one with prosciutto, the other with cream cheese. Another year, our older tree gave us a magnificent crop of small figs. This was the favourite pudding of that summer.

12 small figs
Vanilla sugar

Wash the figs and, while they are still wet, roll them in the sugar so that they are well coated. Place them tightly in a deep oven proof dish and cook in a hot oven (220°C) for about 20 minutes. Check them during cooking. They will be cooked when the sugar has been transformed into a brown juice at the bottom of the dish.

When cold, these can be served with Greek yoghurt or, for fancy work, they can be layered with cream or crème Anglaise (see page 217) and mille feuilles (see page 211) into perhaps the most magnificent dessert of the summer.

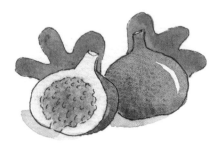

Herbs and Weeds

When inspiration or money is lacking a visit to the herb garden can give solace. The simplest of meals can be created by gathering a handful of herbs. Chinese leaves self-seed, American landcress can be found in all but the driest summers. Borage leaves can be chopped to put into salads and the bright blue flowers used to decorate. The Genoese have a great tradition of cooking borage fritters and mixing borage with Ricotta as a stuffing for ravioli. Omelettes, roasts, marinades, pasta sauce, salads can all be elevated by the addition of herbs. John Evelyn in his *Acetaria, A Discourse of Sallets*, 1699, advised that sorrel be added to every salad as it imparts 'so graceful a quickness to the rest, as supplies the want of orange, limon and other omphacia'. Rosemary transforms lamb and sage is perfect with liver or veal. Milk puddings can be given new directions by flavourings of sweet Cicely, scented geraniums or elderflowers.

Weeds have their uses too. In April, young stinging nettles make wonderful soup and dandelion leaves can be added to salad. Best of all are wild garlic leaves which can be used in place of garlic bulbs in many recipes. Mark Hix is a great fan of wild garlic and gives many ideas on how to use them in his Saturday column in the *Independent*.

I limit this chapter to favourite, special recipes and ideas that are directly inspired by the most abundant herbs and weeds in the garden.

Prawns and Chives Smörgås

This recipe was inspired by a lunch in the Millesgården Museum in Stockholm.

Cooked prawns in a mayonnaise (see page 212) very lightly flavoured (and coloured) with a smidgen of tomato purée and a few drops of tabasco make a wonderful first course when decorated with very finely chopped chives, specks of red chilli, and finely sliced radish. Serve on rye bread.

Egg and Chive Sandwiches

Using the freshest oatmeal loaf, egg and chive sandwiches made with melted butter and seasoned with salt and freshly ground black pepper are sublime.

Sorrel Butter

Take the stalks off a few sorrel leaves and blend in a Liquidiser with some softened butter. Form into a sausage-sized roll and wrap in clingfilm. Place in the fridge for the butter to harden.

To serve, unwrap and cut the butter into slices to place on top of fish.

Rocket or Basil Pesto Sauce

This is so good and can be made with rocket or basil. A handful of rocket or basil, Liquidised with a few cloves of garlic, enough olive oil to form a paste, 75g of grated Parmesan cheese (or Parmesan and Pecorino cheese) and 100g or so of lightly toasted pine nuts. Kept in a jar in the fridge, this sauce will stay fresh for a week. Serve tossed in spaghetti or linguine with extra freshly grated Parmesan to hand.

Sorrel Soufflé

I make one large soufflé but this mixture could also be divided between four ramekins.

40g butter
30g plain flour
A pinch of cayenne pepper
275 ml milk
4 eggs, separated
Handful sorrel leaves, finely chopped
Salt and freshly ground black pepper

Melt the butter in a small saucepan. Remove the pan from the heat and stir in the flour and cayenne pepper. Return to the heat and let the mixture bubble. On a very low heat, gradually stir in the milk to make a smooth sauce. Add the sorrel and let the sauce barely boil for two minutes. Remove from the heat and stir in the egg yolks. Season.

Whisk the egg whites until just stiff. Mix a spoonful of the whites into the sauce to loosen it and, using a metal spoon, carefully fold in the rest of the egg whites.

Place in a well-buttered soufflé dish and put into a hot oven (220°C) for 10 minutes or until the soufflé has risen and has a brown crust on top.

Spinach could be substituted for the sorrel and 75g finely grated Cheddar, Parmesan or Gruyère cheese added to either soufflé.

Horseradish Sauce

We dug some horseradish from the roadside a few miles south of Bath to plant on the allotment and it has been flourishing ever since. It is as well that we use almost enough to stop it from spreading out of control.

Grated horseradish can simply be added to beef stews but this sauce is excellent not only with Sunday roast beef but also fish, especially mackerel, and it is a good addition to smoked fish patés.

50g grated peeled horseradish
4 tbsp soured cream
Black peppercorns

Grating the horseradish is the hard part. I have learnt to do it with my eyes closed. Put the grated horseradish into a basin and mix in the cream and peppercorns which can either be left whole or coarsely ground. For serving with fish, capers could be added.

Parsley-stuffed Portobello Mushrooms

8 large Portobello mushrooms
1 small onion, peeled and finely chopped
2 cloves of garlic, peeled and crushed
200g butter
120g fresh white breadcrumbs
4 tbsp chopped parsley
Salt and freshly ground black pepper

Remove the stalks from the mushrooms and finely chop them. Add to the onion and cook gently in the butter for a few minutes until the onion is soft but not coloured. Add garlic towards the end of cooking. Season. Put the mixture into a food processor and blitz briefly. Add the breadcrumbs and parsley.

Divide the mixture between the mushrooms and stuff lightly. Bake in the oven at 190°C for about 30 minutes until lightly coloured.

Chicken Liver Pâté with Thyme

Thyme is essential for this pâté which could also be made with duck livers.

450g chicken livers
125g butter
2 garlic cloves, pressed
3 sprigs thyme
100 ml sherry
100 ml brandy
50g butter, melted
Salt and freshly ground black pepper

Check over the livers and remove any green bits as they will give a bitter taste. Melt the butter in a heavy frying pan and sauté the livers. Cook them gently until they are brown all over. Add the garlic towards the end of cooking.

Sprinkle over the thyme leaves. Holding back the juices, transfer the livers to a food processor. Return the pan to the heat and add the sherry, brandy, and seasoning to the remaining juices. Cook, letting it bubble for a minute or two, then pour into the processor. Blitz the pâté more or less depending on how coarse you like it to be.

Turn it into a pâté dish and, using a knife, make the top smooth. Melt the smaller amount of butter. Place a sprig of thyme on top of the pâté, then pour over the melted butter.

Let the pâté cool and then keep it in the fridge. It can be made a day or two in advance.

Serve with hot toast.

MINT TEA

Crush slightly four to five mint stems and put them in a warmed teapot. Pour over boiling water. In the Middle East, boiling water is simply poured over stems of mint placed in a glass. If required, sugar or honey could be used as a sweetener.

MINT SAUCE

Handful mint leaves
1 tsp sugar
1 tbsp boiling water
1 tbsp white wine vinegar

Using a pestle and mortar, pound the mint leaves. When very fine, add the sugar and leave for half an hour for the sugar to soak up the juices. Add only enough boiling water to dissolve the sugar and, when cool, add the vinegar. This sauce can be made in advance and stored in a jar, kept in the fridge.

DANDELION SALAD

Tender, young dandelion leaves can be made into the most delicious salad, served warm with pieces of hot smoked streaky bacon.

Prepare the dandelion leaves and place them in a bowl. Using a frying pan, fry the bacon until crisp, then put to one side to keep warm. Add a tablespoon or two of white wine vinegar to the fat in the frying pan and let it bubble for a minute or two. Place the bacon in the salad and then add the sauce. Mix well and serve immediately.

TABBOULEH

A taste of the Middle East. There are lots of different recipes and regional variations. In her book, *Arabesque*, Claudia Roden gives wise advice to finely slice rather than chop the parsley to prevent it from becoming mushy.

60g bulgar wheat
1 large bunch flat-leafed parsley
1 small bunch mint
1 small bunch coriander
Juice of 2 lemons, grated zest of 1 lemon
250g tomatoes, deseeded and finely diced
½ cucumber, finely diced
6 spring onions, thinly sliced
6 tbsp olive oil
Salt and freshly ground black pepper

for serving:
2 Little Gem or Tom Thumb lettuce

Rinse the bulgar wheat in cold water, then strain thoroughly. Place the wheat in a large bowl and add the lemon juice and diced tomatoes. Do this 20 minutes before serving tabbouleh to allow time for the wheat to soften in the juices.

While the bulgar wheat is softening, keeping the parsley in a bunch, wash and dry it, then placing it on a chopping board, slice it very finely. In the same way, prepare the mint and coriander leaves. Prepare the cucumber and spring onions. Stir all the remaining ingredients in with the bulgar wheat, season, and mix well.

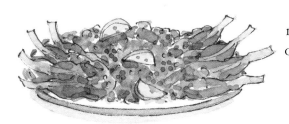

I like to serve tabbouleh in the middle of a deep dish with segments of lettuce protruding on two sides.

Herb Stuffing for Fish

This works really well with fresh sardines.

1 tbsp olive oil
1 onion, peeled and finely chopped
2 cloves garlic, peeled and crushed,
    or a handful of chopped wild garlic leaves
1 tsp cumin
1 tsp ground turmeric
½ tsp ground coriander
Juice of ½ lemon
Salt and freshly ground black pepper
Handful parsley, chopped
1 tbsp chopped coriander

Heat the olive oil in a frying pan and gently cook the onion until soft but not coloured. Add the spices and garlic and cook for a further two minutes.

Remove from the heat and allow to cool. Stir in parsley, coriander and lemon juice. Open the fish, spoon in the stuffing, dust the fish lightly with flour before frying. Serve warm.

NETTLE SOUP

Use only young nettle shoots and be sure to wear very thick gloves.

1 carrier bag young nettle shoots
50g butter
1 large onion, peeled and chopped
2 leeks, washed and sliced
2 celery sticks, sliced
1 large potato, peeled and diced
2 cloves garlic or a few leaves or wild garlic
1 litre vegetable or chicken stock
Salt and freshly ground black pepper
Double cream, crème fraîche or plain yoghurt

Using thick rubber gloves, pick over the nettle leaves in several changes of water. Discard any thick stalks. Leave to drain in a colander.

In a large heavy pan, melt the butter then add the onion, leeks, potato, celery and sweat for five or so minutes. Add the garlic, then the stock and cook until the vegetables are soft. Add the nettle leaves and cook for a few minutes longer. In batches, Liquidise the soup. Season.

Serve hot with a spoonful of cream, crème fraîche or yoghurt swirled on the top of each bowl.

PARMESAN AND THYME STRAWS

150g Parmesan cheese, freshly grated
1 tsp thyme leaves
½ tsp ground paprika
20 stoned black olives, finely chopped
Salt and freshly ground black pepper
250g puff pastry (all butter ready-made
   would be fine for this recipe)
1 egg, beaten

Put the Parmesan cheese, thyme leaves, paprika, olives, salt, and pepper into a bowl and stir.

Roll out the pastry on a floured surface to about 15 x 30 cm. Brush with a little beaten egg and sprinkle with a third of the cheese mixture, spread evenly all over the pastry. Fold the bottom third of the pastry up and the top third down to cover it. Roll out as before and repeat the process twice with the remaining mixture. Finish by rolling the pastry into a 20 x 30 cm rectangle. Brush with the remaining beaten egg.

Starting parallel with one of the shorter ends, cut the pastry into about 20 strips, 1-2 cm wide. Either leave plain or twist the strips into spirals and place them on a baking tray lined with a lightly oiled baking sheet. Bake for 10-12 minutes with the oven heated to 200°C or until risen and golden brown.

Cool slightly, then place on a wire rack. Serve warm.

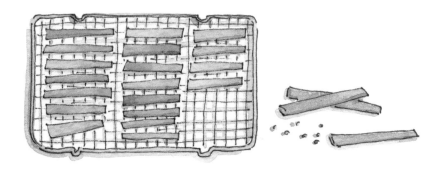

LEEKS

L eeks are the stars of the winter allotment. Musselborough are my favourites, short but solid. Grown from seed, by mid-July they are pencil size and ready to be trimmed top and bottom and planted out into rows of spacious deep holes.

Mud can be found well down in the white part of leeks so careful washing is required before cooking with them. If the leeks are to be finely sliced, it is often a good idea to give them a final wash before use.

Leeks require little spicing; with butter, cheese or cream, their flavour stands by itself. Chives are a better decoration than parsley and crusty bread the perfect accompaniment.

Your majesty says very true: if your majesties is remembered of it, the Welshmen did good service in a garden where leeks did grow, wearing leeks in their Monmouth caps; which, your majesty know, to this hour is an honourable badge of the service; and I do believe your majesty takes no scorn to wear the leek upon Saint Tavy's day.

William Shakespeare,
King Henry V,
Act 1, scene 4

Vichyssoise

My leeks are not ready in midsummer but this soup is a treat for balmy autumn days when eating outside is still possible.

8 leeks, white parts only
900ml good chicken stock
2/3 potatoes, peeled and chopped
300ml double cream
Salt and freshly ground black pepper
A small bunch chives, snipped

Wash and chop the leeks. Simmer in the chicken stock in a covered pan for 10 minutes. Add the potatoes, salt and pepper and cook for a further 20 minutes. Liquidise, strain through a sieve and cool. Add the cream, check the seasoning and chill. Serve in cold bowls and garnish with the chives.

Everyday Leeks

Trim and wash leeks. Cut larger ones in half and slice. Put into a pan with equal quantities of water and olive oil, enough to not quite cover the leeks and cook gently for about 10 minutes until the leeks are soft. Stir occasionally and check the liquid.

Add more water if the pan is drying. It shouldn't be necessary to drain the leeks but serve them immediately with the scant liquid that is left. A little salt should be added before the end of cooking.

Leek Tart (Tarte aux Poireaux)

300g quiche pastry (see page 209)
6/7 medium leeks, trimmed, washed and sliced
150g butter
300ml double cream
4 egg yolks
Salt and freshly ground black pepper

Cook the leeks gently in the butter with a tablespoon of salted water until they are soft. This may take 30 minutes but it is important not to rush and never let them brown. Drain and allow to cool.

Roll out the pastry large enough to line a 22cm diameter flan dish and, picking it up by the sides, position the pastry in the dish, firming it into the corners lightly and pressing on the top of the case to discourage the sides from collapsing. To this end, it may help to also moisten the top edge of the flan case before pressing down the pastry. Keep in a cool place for a further 20 minutes before baking blind in a medium oven.

Whisk the egg yolks with the cream and seasoning and add the leeks. Pour into the prepared pastry base. Bake for about 25 minutes in a medium oven (180°C) until the filling has set and coloured just a little.

A good variation is to add about three tablespoons of Parmesan cheese to the egg mixture before baking.

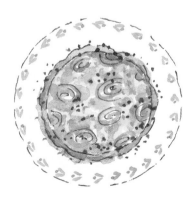

Leek Pie (Flamiche)

My take on the famous pie from Picardy.

350g puff pastry, bought or home-made (see pages 210-11)
50g butter
6/7 leeks, trimmed, sliced and washed
75g cream cheese
4 tbsp double cream
A pinch grated nutmeg
1 tbsp Parmesan cheese, grated
1 egg yolk, beaten
1 tbsp snipped chives (optional)
Salt and freshly ground black pepper

Using very cold puff pastry cut in half and roll the halves out to make two thin squares with sides approximately 25cm in length. Place one square on a buttered baking sheet, cover with clingfilm and put the other square on top. Cover and chill for at least 20 minutes.

In a pan, melt the butter and add the leeks. Cook gently for about 30 minutes until they are soft but not coloured. Allow to cool. In a bowl whisk together the cream cheese, double cream, nutmeg, chives (if using), salt and pepper. Add the leeks.

Place one rectangle of pastry onto a baking tray. Spread the filling over it leaving a 2cm edge. Scatter over the Parmesan cheese and, using a pastry brush, 'paint' the edges with the beaten egg yolk.

Place the second square over the first, pressing the edges together with a fork. Tidy the seams if necessary by cutting off odd bits of pastry and making the edges straight. Make slits in the top crust to allow the steam to escape and, using a knife, score the pastry, making a crisscross pattern on the crust. Brush the top with the remaining egg yolk.

Bake at 200°C for 35-40 minutes or until the pie is golden brown, puffed and crisp.

Allow to cool for a few minutes before cutting into wedges and serving.

Welsh Rarebit Leeks

8 leeks, trimmed and left whole
150g Caerphilly cheese, grated
2 egg yolks
3 tsp Worcestershire sauce

1 tsp mustard powder
80ml beer
80ml double cream
Salt and freshly ground black pepper

Cook the leeks in boiling salted water for about eight minutes, until almost tender. Simmer the beer until it has reduced by half. Add the cream and continue simmering until this is thick. Add remaining ingredients and taste. Arrange leeks on an ovenproof dish. Spoon over the sauce and place under a grill or in a hot oven until golden.

This makes a good lunch dish to be served with fresh bread and a green salad.

Leeks Vinaigrette

It is important to have everything right for this dish in order to avoid rubbery or stringy consequences. Only very fresh young leeks should be used.

16 young leeks
1 tbsp Dijon mustard
Salt and freshly ground black
  pepper

1 tbsp white wine vinegar
250 ml or less light olive oil
2 hard-boiled eggs
1 tbsp chives, snipped

Trim and wash the leeks and cook in salted water for 10 minutes. Drain well (saving a very little of the boiling water) and allow to cool.

To make the dressing; using a whisk, blend the mustard, salt, pepper, vinegar and add the oil slowly. Taste. The dressing should be the consistency of single cream and can be thinned by adding a teaspoon of the saved water.

Cut the leeks in half. Arrange on a dish. Pour over enough of the dressing and decorate with finely chopped boiled eggs and chives.

LEEK FRITTERS WITH SOURED CREAM DRESSING

4-5 leeks, trimmed, halved lengthways, thinly sliced and washed
Good pinch salt
3 spring onions, trimmed, halved lengthways and finely sliced
30g plain flour
1 tsp baking powder
Freshly ground black pepper
Pinch cayenne pepper
1 egg
Rapeseed oil for frying
1 small tub soured cream
2 tbsp chives, snipped
A pinch of paprika or sumac

Cook the sliced leeks in boiling salted water for about four minutes or until they begin to soften. Drain and wring them out in a kitchen towel.

In a large bowl, whisk the flour and baking powder with the egg, then add salt, peppers, spring onions and the leeks and stir.

Heat a few tablespoons of oil into a pan. In batches, as they will need space, drop in tablespoons of the leek mixture, flattening them with the back of a spoon. Cook for about three minutes on each side. As they are cooked, transfer them to a warm dish lined with kitchen paper and keep them in a warm oven until all batches are prepared and ready to serve.

Serve with soured cream, flavoured with chives, paprika or sumac.

LETTUCE

'Lettuce be grateful!' is the cry in summer when lettuce is plentiful. It is good to grow different types in sequence in short rows. With careful planning, lettuce can last from late spring until November. Without a greenhouse, the earliest plants are best bought as seedlings from garden centres. Cos is a favourite and the hardy varieties such as Little Gem and Tom Thumb are always useful. I also like to mix colours in my salad crop by including red tinged leaves. Increasingly seed suppliers are offering packs of mixed salad leaves.

Gerard, in the seventeenth century, had the common problem of when to serve the salad.

It is served in these days, and in these countries
in the beginning of supper, and eaten first before any other meat: which
also Martial testifieth to be done in his time, marvelling why some did
use it for a service at the end of supper, in these verses.

Tell me why Lettuce, which our Grandsires last did eate,
Is now of late become, to be the first of meat?

Notwithstanding it may now and then be eaten at both
those times to the health of the body: for being taken before meat it doth
many times stir up appetite: and eaten after supper it keepeth away
drunkennesse which commeth by the wine; and that is by reason that it
staieth the vapours from rising up into the head.

John Gerard,
Herball or Generall Historie of Plantes,
3rd ed. 1636.

CHILLED LETTUCE AND CELERY SOUP

A refreshing soup that makes a good starter for an al fresco lunch.

2 tbsp olive oil
2 leeks, cut into small pieces and washed
3 sticks of celery cut into small pieces
1 onion, peeled and roughly chopped
1 tbsp plain flour
1 litre vegetable stock
4 heads of small lettuce
A few lovage leaves
Salt and freshly ground black pepper
2-3 tbsp double cream

Gently cook the leeks, celery and onion in the olive oil until soft. Add flour and stir well with a wooden spoon over a low heat for a minute or so. Slowly add the vegetable stock and, continuing to stir, bring to the boil. Season with salt and pepper and simmer for 20 minutes. Add the lettuces and the lovage leaves, remembering that lovage has a very strong flavour. Remove from the heat and blend in Liquidiser until smooth. Strain through a fine mesh. Check seasoning. Allow to cool and, lastly stir in the cream.

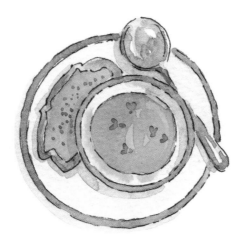

LETTUCE AND PEA SOUP

✦

40g butter

1 onion, finely chopped

1 large or two small lettuces, shredded

1 tbsp plain flour

225g shelled peas

450 ml chicken stock

450 ml full milk

2 egg yolks

75 ml single cream

Salt and freshly ground black pepper

Sprigs of mint

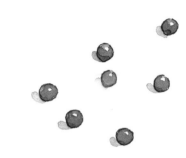

Melt the butter in a large saucepan and add the onion and lettuce. Cook gently in a covered pan, stirring occasionally for 10 minutes. Stir in the flour. Continue stirring and add the peas. Pour in the stock and milk and bring to the boil, then reduce the heat to a scant simmer and cook for 20 minutes. Season and, optionally, add a few mint leaves. Purée the soup, then pass through a sieve. Return to the pan. Mix the egg yolks with the cream and blend into the soup. Heat through but do not allow to boil.

Serve hot, garnished with mint leaves.

Lettuce Salad

Mixed leaves freshly picked are nothing like the bags of leaves available in supermarkets. By careful picking to thin the plantings, using small outside leaves, and mixing in herbs or other salad leaves, such as rocket and cress, the most perfect salad is made with all sorts of tastes coming from the leaves themselves.

Wash the leaves very carefully, as there will be slugs, greenfly and soil hidden, then dry them either in a salad dryer or by wrapping the leaves in a tea towel and giving it a good shake. Dressings must vary depending on the spiciness or flavour of the leaves but I give my basic recipe.

2 tbsp olive oil (or rapeseed oil)
1 tbsp white wine vinegar
Generous pinch English mustard
   powder or ½ tsp Dijon mustard

Scant pinch granulated sugar
Garlic, pressed or finely chopped
Salt and freshly ground black
   pepper.

Place all the ingredients in a jar with lid and shake vigorously. Pour as much as required over the salad which has been placed in a large bowl and, immediately before serving, *fatigue la salade* by gently turning over the leaves until they are all coated.

Blue Cheese Salad Dressing

I admit to being a purist when it comes to salad dressing and do not need it to have many ingredients. This dressing is very good served at lunch time. Cream cheese could be used in place of the blue cheese and cream.

150g creamy blue cheese
Juice and zest of one lemon
2 tbsp olive oil
1 tbsp double cream
Salt and freshly ground black pepper

Mix all the ingredients together in a blender and dress the salad as in the previous recipe. Walnuts and slices of pears would be a welcome addition.

ANCHOVY AND EGG DRESSING

Another recipe from my friend Penny Dalrymple-Smith

4 tbsp sunflower oil or other simple oil
1 tbsp lemon juice or white wine vinegar
1 clove garlic
2 anchovies
1 egg yolk
Salt and freshly ground black pepper

Put all the ingredients in a blender and blend until smooth.

This can be left as a simple dressing for lettuce or made into a luncheon dish by laying out the dressed lettuce on a serving dish and adding croutons, quartered hard boiled eggs, and strips of anchovy on top.

STEAMED PEAS AND LETTUCE

Once more, thanks to Louise Pavey for this recipe. Peas harvested towards the end of the season can be dry but, by cooking them in this way, they become tender and moist.

Line the container of the steamer with lettuce leaves and spread over the peas. Steam for about 10 minutes or until the peas are soft.

Serve hot. I like to shake over a little light soya sauce.

ONIONS AND SHALLOTS

Onions, the most popular of all vegetables, are nearly always used in conjunction with other ingredients. Along with beans and cabbages, they were the first cultivated vegetable. In ancient Egypt they were considered an object to worship, their shape and concentric rings symbolizing eternal life. Greek athletes ate large quantities believing that onions lightened the balance of the blood and Roman gladiators were rubbed down with onions to firm their muscles.

Less perishable than most vegetables, in the Middle Ages onions were sometimes used as currency. An onion in a stockpot or broth must have been a welcome addition, worth paying for. Thyme and sage are my favourite herbs with onion, Lancashire and Gruyère my favourite cheeses.

The flavour of shallots is more delicate and sweet. I prefer them to onions raw in salads and find they have a special affinity with mussels.

Shrek: *For your information, there's a lot more to ogres than people think.*
Donkey: *Example?*
Shrek: *Example... uh... ogres are like onions!*
Donkey: *They stink?*
Shrek: *Yes... No!*
Donkey: *Oh, they make you cry?*
Shrek: *No!*
Donkey: *Oh, you leave 'em out in the sun, they get all brown, start sproutin' little white hairs...*
Shrek: *NO! Layers. Onions have layers. Ogres have layers. Onions have layers. You get it? We both have layers.*

Shrek (2001) Directors Andrew Adamson and Vicky Jenson, writer (book) William Steig, (screenplay) Ted Elliott

FRENCH ONION SOUP

This is such a warming soup, I cannot think of it without an image of steam rising and cheese melting. Everything seems to be to hand to make this soup in the early days of January.

4 large onions, sliced very thinly
30g butter
1 tbsp olive oil
Small pinch brown sugar
½ tsp Dijon mustard
1.5 ml good stock, preferably beef
½ glass red wine (optional)
4-6 slices French bread
100g grated Gruyère or Emmental cheese
Salt and freshly ground black pepper

In a heavy pan on a low heat, melt the butter with the olive oil. Add the onions and cook them gently, stirring occasionally with a wooden spoon, for about 20 minutes or until they turn opaque and begin to soften, then add the sugar and continue to cook, letting the onions turn an even rich brown colour. Take care not to let them stick to the bottom of the pan or burn.

Add the stock and wine (if using). Bring to the boil and then let the soup simmer, with the pan covered, for about 30 minutes. Just before serving add the mustard and season to taste.

Put the bread slices on a roasting tray, sprinkle with a generous serving of grated cheese, and toast in the oven until the bread begins to brown and the cheese is melted. Place a slice of the toasted bread in the bottom of each soup bowl and ladle the hot soup into the bowls.

Serve piping hot.

PISSALADIÈRE

There are so many versions of onion tarts I feel justified in including two, one French inspired and the other from the north of England. Either is perfect for lunch, served warm, not hot, with a simple green salad.

1 sheet butter puff pastry
6 medium sized onions, peeled and thinly sliced
2 tomatoes, skinned, deseeded and chopped
3 tbsp olive oil
A few black olives, stoned
6-7 anchovy fillets
Salt and pepper
Milk to brush pastry

Using a large frying pan with a lid, gently cook the onions in the olive oil for about 20 minutes. Keep the lid on for the last 10 minutes but check frequently as the onions must not burn.

Add the tomatoes and cook gently, still with lid on, for another 10 minutes until the mixture is well amalgamated. Add salt (not too much because anchovies will be added later) and a generous amount of black pepper. Leave to cool.

While the onions are cooling, roll out puff pastry into a rectangle and take off a small triangle in each corner with a sharp knife. With a straight ruler (I use a small chopping board) and knife, score down the pastry about two centimeters in from the edge on each side. Lightly brush the edges of the pastry with milk and turn up the margins to form a lip. Transfer the pastry carefully to a greased baking tray, spread the onion mixture over the pastry base and decorate with the anchovies to form a diagonal pattern. Place a black olive in the centre of each diamond.

Cook for about 20 minutes at 180/190°C until the pastry is golden brown.

Lancashire Cheese and Onion Pie

This recipe evolved from one published in *Simon Hopkinson Cooks*.

300g rich short crust pastry either bought or made (see p. 214)

For the filling:

25g butter
6 medium onions, peeled and roughly sliced
250g Lancashire cheese, coarsely grated
Salt and freshly ground white pepper
Milk for sealing and glazing

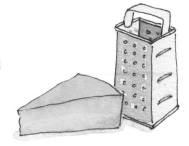

Have the pastry ready and keeping cool in the fridge.

To make the filling, heat the butter in a heavy based saucepan and add the onions. Fry gently for 15 minutes so they are soft but not coloured. Add 150 ml water and season with salt and white pepper. Continue cooking gently until almost all the water has evaporated. This may take 20 minutes. Turn out into a dish to cool.

Roll out two-thirds of the pastry and use to line a greased 20cm diameter loose-bottomed tart tin. Spoon half of the onions into the pie base, spread over the grated cheese, and spoon the remainder of the onions on top. Roll out the rest of the pastry to form the pie lid.

Moisten the edges of the base with milk, place the pie lid over the pie and press down the edges. Using a knife, tidy the edges and make an incision in the centre of the pie. Decorate the top using spare pastry. Finally, brush over with milk and bake at 180°C for about 40 minutes until golden brown. To make sure that the base of the pie is cooked, place it on the bottom of the oven for 10 minutes of the cooking time. Leave for a few minutes before turning out and serving in slices.

BALSAMIC ROASTED RED ONIONS

4 red onions, peeled and cut into quarters

6 tbsp balsamic vinegar

4 tbsp olive oil

2 tbsp light brown sugar

A bunch of fresh oregano, roughly chopped

1 clove garlic, crushed

1 tsp sesame seeds (optional)

Salt and pepper

In a bowl, mix the balsamic vinegar, olive oil, sugar, oregano, and seasoning.

Place onion wedges in a roasting tin and spoon the balsamic mixture over, turning the onion wedges until they are coated. Bake in an oven heated to 190°C for 20 minutes. Turn the onions, sprinkle over the sesame seeds (if using), and cook for a further 15 minutes or until the onions are soft and sticky. Add the crushed garlic.

Serve warm with a steak and green salad.

SHALLOT AND TOMATO SALAD

The sweetness of the shallots combines well with tomatoes.

1 shallot, peeled and finely chopped

4 tomatoes, finely sliced

1 tbsp parsley, finely chopped

2 tbsp red wine vinegar

4 tbsp olive oil

4 tbsp crème fraîche

Salt and freshly ground black pepper

Arrange the tomatoes in a shallow bowl. Combine all the other ingredients and pour over.

Serve immediately.

MOULES MARINIÈRES

2kg mussels
2 tbsp olive oil
1 clove garlic, crushed
1 medium onion, peeled and finely chopped
3 shallots, peeled and finely chopped
1 bunch parsley
100g crème fraîche
1 glass white wine

Carefully check the mussels and discard any that are open. Remove any beards and clean the mussels thoroughly in cold water.

In a large casserole, heat the olive oil and sauté the onion and shallots for a few minutes. Then add the parsley and garlic and cook for a further minute or two.

Add the mussels and cover the pot. Cook gently for 15 minutes before adding the white wine and letting the mussels simmer for five minutes more. Stir in the crème fraîche just before serving in warmed bowls.

PARSNIPS

The first time I tried to grow parsnips I carefully put single seeds into a row of spaced out drills that been filled with sand. What might have happened I do not know as, seeing what seemed like an empty space, they were dug over and the ground prepared for another crop. Parsnips do take an age to germinate. Subsequent trials have been more successful. I have also learned to plant lettuce as a catch crop between the drills. On an abandoned allotment near my own, a high row of flowering parsnips forms a delicate hedge.

The parsnip is closely related to the carrot and they go well together. One curious thing about parsnips is that, as sweet as they are, a little sugar or honey does much to intensify their flavour. It is a winter vegetable and its flavour is improved by leaving it in the ground until after the early frosts.

The parsnip is native to Britain. It must have been grown in France and Germany in Roman times as supplies were set to the Emperor Tiberius but parsnips have never truly been adopted in European cooking.

Wild parsnips can still be found growing on chalky grassland and roadsides. It is a biennial plant with attractive chrome yellow umbels and sweet smelling seeds that were collected for medical use.

Parsnip wine should be the tipple of every allotment holder. In the eighteenth century it was a fashionable drink, often substituted for Madeira to which it was compared in taste.

"Faire words butter noe parsnips".

The earliest example of this expression, according to
The Oxford English Dictionary, is dated 1639.

Parsnip, Carrot and Bulgar Wheat Salad

Cut parsnips and carrots into batons and then spread out, tossed in a little olive oil and salted and roasted in a hot oven for 20 minutes until soft and beginning to brown.

Meanwhile soften about 100g or more of bulgar wheat in a bowl with skinned, chopped tomatoes and lemon juice.

Let the parsnips and carrots cool. Assemble a salad by mixing the bulgar wheat with the roasted vegetables and adding Feta cheese, young mint leaves, chopped parsley and tossing all the ingredients in a salad dressing made from four parts olive oil to two of lemon juice and one of honey, salt, pepper, a pinch of ground cumin and, optionally, half a teaspoon or less of harissa paste.

Warm Winter Vegetable Salad

This salad makes an ideal first course.

Cut peeled parsnips, beetroot, carrots, sweet potatoes and squashes into different shaped cubes and put into a roasting dish together with a few whole, skinned shallots and peeled cloves of garlic. Toss the vegetables around in a little olive oil and roast in a hot oven for about 25 minutes or until the vegetables are soft and begin to turn brown. Take the dish out of the oven from time to time to check on the vegetables and stir them around.

Make a dressing from the juice of half a pomegranate, two tablespoons olive oil, one of balsamic vinegar, salt and freshly ground black pepper. A spoonful of pomegranate syrup should also be added to the dressing but warm honey mixed with a little lemon juice could be used in its place.

Shake the dressing well before tasting and pouring it carefully over the hot vegetables. Scatter over pomegranate seeds from the remaining half of the pomegranate before serving.

PARSNIP, CHICKPEA AND SAFFRON SOUP

This recipe is based on an item about chickpeas in the *Cook* section of a Saturday edition of *The Guardian*. I have added the onion and olive oil.

I small onion, finely sliced
2 tbsp olive oil
250g parsnips, peeled and cubed
750ml chicken stock
400g tin chickpeas, (or cooked equivalent), drained
Pinch ground cumin
Pinch saffron
2 tbsp milk
125ml double cream
Snipped chives to garnish

In a casserole gently fry the onion in the oil until opaque but not coloured. Add the parsnips and the chicken stock. Cover and gently boil the parsnips until tender. Add the chickpeas and cook for a further five minutes. Season and add the cumin.

Soak the saffron in the milk. Blend the soup to a purée and return it to the pan. Add the saffron and the cream and heat through gently but do not let it boil.

Serve immediately with the chives scattered on top.

MASHED PARSNIPS AND CARROTS

Boil parsnips and carrots separately in salted water then drain and mash them together with plenty of butter, black pepper and chopped parsley. A pinch of nutmeg could also be added.

SAUTÉED PARSNIPS

Peel the parsnips and take off their tops and straggly ends. Cut into halves or quarters Boil them in salted water for 10 minutes. Drain, then gently sauté the parsnips in butter until soft and light golden brown. Serve with chopped parsley and a squeeze of lemon.

PARSNIP CRISPS

4 medium parsnips, scrubbed clean
Corn oil
Sea salt

Top and tail the parsnips. Leaving on the skin, slice lengthways with a potato peeler or mandoline. Dry on kitchen paper.

Heat about 8 cm of corn oil in a deep fryer or heavy based saucepan. Heat oil and test with one slice. Deep fry the slices a handful at a time for about 3 minutes. When they are ready, remove and drain on kitchen paper. Season while still hot with sea salt.

Beetroot can be prepared in the same way.

PARSNIPS MOLLY PARKIN

Thanks to Bärbl Gascoigne for introducing me to this dish which has become a firm favourite. I like to serve it with grilled meat and a watercress salad.

750g parsnips
450g tomatoes
4 tbsp olive oil
50g butter
1 tbsp soft brown sugar
Salt and freshly ground black pepper
200 ml single cream
125g Gruyère cheese, grated
4 tbsp white breadcrumbs
1 tbsp thyme leaves

Take off the tops and bottoms of the parsnips, peel them, slice in half and cut out any hard central cores. Slice thinly. Skin tomatoes and cut the flesh into rough slices.

Heat the oil in a pan and lightly fry the parsnips for four minutes.

Grease a casserole dish generously with butter. Place half the parsnips over the base. Sprinkle with a little sugar, some thyme leaves, and season generously. Add a little cream before covering with a layer of tomatoes, then more cream and half of the grated Gruyère. Repeat these layers, finishing with cream and cheese. Top with breadcrumbs and dot with butter. Bake in a moderate oven (160°C) for 40-60 minutes or until the top is golden and the parsnips are tender. If the top becomes too brown before the parsnips are ready, cover loosely with tin foil.

PEARS

There is something very French about pears. Espaliered trees, ripening fruit protected in bags growing in bottles; all very ordered. By the 17th century, pears were the supreme fruit of the age. De la Quintinie, gardener to King Louis XIV, grew over 30 varieties of pear in the Potager du Roi at Versailles. Louis's favourite was Bon Chrétien. He regularly made gifts of the pear to visiting foreign dignitaries.

The King had a party trick and could peel a pear in such a way that the skin could be put back in place, giving the appearance of a whole fruit.

We grow three types of pear on the allotment, Bon Chrétien, Dr Jules Guyot and the 'pear drop' pear, Jargonelle. Our trees are untidy but the fruit is delicious. I believe the truism that a pear is only perfect for 10 minutes. Perfect (or near perfect pears) are delicious as a starter with Parma ham or a creamy blue cheese.

Pears discolour quickly. To prevent this, have a bowl of lemon juice in water to hand in which to place the prepared fruit.

PEAR AND BLUE CHEESE SALAD

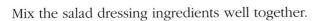

"Do not let the peasants know how good pears are with cheese."
an Italian saying.

Anna del Conte, *Italian Kitchen.*

4 ripe pears
200g creamy blue cheese such as Bath Blue, Per Las or Cashel Blue
3 tbsp olive oil
2 tbsp lemon juice
1 tsp honey (optional)
120g rocket
Salt and freshly ground black pepper

Mix the salad dressing ingredients well together.

Peel and core the pears then cut them into eighths. Place in a bowl with half the salad dressing and leave for an hour. Share the rocket out among four serving plates, put the pear slices on top and then small broken bits of cheese. Finish with a gentle sprinkling of the remaining salad dressing.

Serve immediately. If the pears are hard, cut them into thin slices and griddle them for a minute or two on each side. This will not only soften them but enhance their sweetness.

Springfield Cake
(Pear and Ginger Sponge)

This pudding has the most impeccable pedigree. It appears in Jane Grigson's *Fruit Book* and then, with full acknowledgement, in Simon Hopkinson's *Second Helpings of Roast Chicken*, where he calls it 'Yummo-scrummo beyond belief'. Hopkinson adds ground ginger to the sponge and accompanies it with a ginger wine flavoured cream. I list these additions as optional. My only change is to blend the crystallized ginger with the eggs so that the sponge is smoother.

For the top:
90g butter
90g granulated sugar
2 tbsp syrup from a jar
   of preserved ginger
Up to 6 firm pears

For the sponge:
125g softened butter
125g caster sugar
100g self-raising flour
1 tsp baking powder
1 tsp ground ginger (optional)
30g ground almonds
2 large eggs
3-4 tbsp syrup from a jar
   of preserved ginger
4 knobs of preserved ginger

Use a nonstick 23-25cm cake tin and put it on the top of the oven over a gentle heat. Add the butter. When it has started to melt, add the sugar and ginger syrup and cook until the ingredients are fused, bubbling and toffee like. Remove from the heat.

Peel, core and slice the pears into eighths, putting the pieces into lemon water as you work. Arrange them in a sunflower pattern on top of the toffee base.

Cream the butter and sugar together, blend the crystalized ginger with the eggs and ginger syrup until smooth. Add all the cake ingredients to the creamed butter and beat well. Pour the cake mixture over the pears and smooth the surface with a knife.

Bake at 180°C for 45 minutes or until the cake is cooked. Keep a check on the top of the cake. If it is becoming too brown, cover with a sheet of tin foil. The cake is done when the edges have started to shrink away from the sides of the tin. If in doubt, leave it in the oven for a little longer, bearing in mind that the bottom ingredients are molten.

Leave for 10 minutes before easing the cake's edges and inverting it onto a large plate.

Serve warm with cream with the optional addition of ginger wine and caster sugar.

PEARS IN RED WINE

This is really good at Christmas time. There must be a myriad of recipes for pears poached in wine but this indulgent recipe which appears in Carolyn Hart's *Cooks' Books* is my favourite.

4-6 hard medium sized pears
Several strips of lemon zest
1 vanilla pod, split lengthways
2 sticks cinnamon
A few cloves and a star anise
110-175g caster sugar
1 bottle of red wine

Peel the pears carefully, leaving on the stems, putting them in lemon water as they are prepared.

Put the wine in a saucepan with the sugar and all the other ingredients and heat slowly until the sugar is dissolved. Add the pears and bring to the boil, then reduce the heat and leave to poach gently until the pears are tender and translucent (this can take from 1 to 4 hours). Take out the pears and place them in a serving dish. Boil the remaining liquid until it is reduced to being thickened and syrupy. Pour it over the pears.

Allow to cool and serve with any sort of cream, according to your taste.

A delicious alternative would be to poach pears in sweetened white wine, flavoured with crushed cardamom pods, saffron and a little lemon juice.

Pear and Apple Chutney

A good recipe for windfalls.

2 kilo net weight pears and apples, peeled, cored and cut into chunks.
250g onion, sliced and chopped
200g raisins
100g sliced stem ginger (or pickled ginger available from
    Chinese supermarkets)
3 cloves garlic, chopped
30g salt
Grated rind and juice of one lemon
350g brown sugar
1tsp cayenne pepper
3-4 cloves, tied in a muslin bag
750ml cider vinegar
250ml distilled malt vinegar

Put the pears and apples, in a large bowl together with the onions, raisins, ginger, garlic, salt and lemon. Put the sugar, spices and vinegar into a pan and boil for 3-4 minutes. Pour over the contents of the bowl and leave overnight.

The next day, boil gently for 3-4 hours until the chutney is dark and rich. Remove the muslin bag before potting in the usual way.

PEAS

Well, fare thee well. I have known thee these twenty-nine years, come peascod time, but an honester and truer-hearted man – well, fare thee well.

William Shakespeare,
Henry IV, Part 2, Act 2, scene 4

For Mistress Quickly 'peascod' time was clearly that moment of the year when peas would have been harvested, podded and dried. It was Clarence Birdseye (1886 – 1956) who, while working as a naturalist in northern Canada, became aware of the advantages of fast freezing and revolutionized the frozen food industry.

Like broad beans, peas can be sown in the autumn for an early crop or in the spring. They are a surprisingly delicate vegetable and like the soil and the air of Eastern England.

Peas go well with ham, mint and lettuce. A few peas can transform minestrone soup, a mid-week risotto and give sweetness and colour to curries and Italian veal stews. I am not ashamed to use frozen peas for some of the sturdier recipes but still love to add just a few fresh peas to many dishes and collect the pods for use as I would hedgerow fruit. I like peas best in a summer vegetable stew of tomatoes, onions, broad beans and artichokes.

In winter a crop of pea shoots can be grown on porous paper kept damp with rain water for use in salads and stir fries.

Pea and Lovage Soup

Lovage is a great flavour to introduce with peas. It has a slight celery smell and grows tall with fine shaped leaves. I don't often use it but it is great in this soup and lovely to have as a high back plant in the herb area.

2 leeks, roughly chopped and
  washed
A good knob of butter
1 litre vegetable stock
400g (shelled weight) peas

8-10 sprigs of lovage
Salt and freshly ground black
  pepper
Crème fraîche

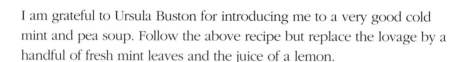

    In a saucepan, gently cook the leeks in the butter for about four minutes or until soft. Add the stock and simmer for a few minutes. Add the peas and continue cooking for a further 10 minutes, adding the lovage in the last minute. Season. Liquidise and strain if you want a very smooth soup. Serve hot with a knob of crème fraîche.

Cold Pea and Mint Soup

I am grateful to Ursula Buston for introducing me to a very good cold mint and pea soup. Follow the above recipe but replace the lovage by a handful of fresh mint leaves and the juice of a lemon.

    Chill well for at least three hours before serving. Decorate with tender mint leaves placed on top of the crème fraîche.

Purée of Fresh Peas

To a kilo of peas cooked in salted water and puréed in a blender add a big knob of butter, black pepper, a few small leaves of mint and a little double cream. Heat in a double boiler. Delicious with veal or gammon and a good way to use peas past their best.

Sformato of Peas

Gently mix 500g of puréed peas as prepared in the previous recipe into 300ml of thick béchamel sauce flavoured with grated Parmesan. Fold in three eggs, whisked, and then turn into a well-buttered ring mould, lined with buttered parchment paper and dusted with dried breadcrumbs. Place the mould into a baking tin filled high with hot water and bake at 190°C for about 45 minutes or until the sformato is firm to the touch..

Turn out carefully onto a plate and serve warm with a tomato sauce poured over.

Peas with Prosciutto

1 medium onion, finely chopped
125g preferably thicker cut prosciutto, cut into strips
4 tbsp olive oil
500g shelled peas
100ml vegetable stock
A bunch of parsley, finely chopped
Salt and freshly ground black pepper

Gently fry the onion in the oil for a few minutes, then add the prosciutto and continue to fry until the onion is golden. Add all the other ingredients, holding back some of the stock, and cook for about 15 minutes or until the peas are tender. Add the reserved stock if the mixture begins to look dry.

PEA AND MINT RISOTTO

Variations on risotto are infinite but this makes a lovely summer supper dish.

1 medium onion, finely chopped
2 cloves garlic, finely chopped
2 tbsp olive oil
Large knob butter
400g risotto rice
150ml white wine
1 litre chicken stock
450g podded peas
25g freshly grated Parmesan cheese
Small bunch fresh mint, chopped
2 tbsp Mascarpone cheese
Salt and freshly ground black pepper

Blanch the peas in salted water for about three minutes. Drain. Heat a large heavy frying pan and add olive oil and butter. When the butter is foaming add the onion and cook gently for 5 minutes until the onion begins to soften. Do not let it brown. Add the garlic and rice. Stir, so that the rice is coated in the oil and cook for a minute. Add the wine then begin to add the chicken stock, a ladleful at a time, allowing the rice to absorb each ladleful before adding more. Do not over stir. In the last minutes of cooking add the peas and then remove from heat before adding Mascarpone, mint and Parmesan. Season well.

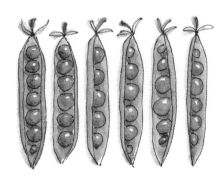

CANNELLONI WITH PEAS AND GORGONZOLA

For the cannelloni:

8 pieces of good quality cannelloni
500ml double cream
50g Parmesan cheese
Salt and freshly ground black pepper
80g Gorgonzola, cut into small cubes
2 egg yolks

For the pea purée:

A good knob of butter
A small onion, finely chopped
500g podded weight of fresh or frozen peas
90ml vegetable stock
A few sprigs of mint
Salt and freshly ground black pepper

To make the pea purée: heat the butter in a pan and gently cook the onion until soft. Add peas, a little of the vegetable stock and mint leaves, season and simmer for 10-12 minutes. Blend in a food processor until smooth. Check the seasoning. The mixture should be fairly stiff.

Meanwhile, bring the double cream to the boil and simmer until it has reduced in volume by two thirds. Add the Parmesan and stir until dissolved. Take off the heat, season and, when cool, whisk in the egg yolks.

Cook the cannelloni until it is 'al dente', refresh in cold water and drain. Fill the cannelloni with the pea purée and place in a dish. Mix the pieces of Gorgonzola with the sauce and pour it over the cannelloni.

Bake in a hot oven for 10-15 minutes or until golden.

PLUMS AND GREENGAGES

I love plums and we freeze a great number of lightly stewed plums to eat at breakfast throughout the year. Herefordshire and Worcestershire are where I think of plum orchards but France too has a long history of growing plums. Of the early fruiting varieties, I am most familiar with River's Early Prolific. Pershore Egg and Pershore Purple come later and Marjorie's Seedling is ripe in September. Most famous of all is the Victoria which produces heavy crops and can be planted in almost any location. Oullin's Gage is a large dual purpose golden gage-plum that would be a good choice for a small garden.

Greengages have an intense flavour and are much sweeter than plums. They are natives of a warmer climate, many coming from Italy via Blois in the Loire valley and home to Claude, wife of François I, after whom several varieties are named. In Britain, greengages can often be found growing well against south facing walls in old kitchen gardens. I have never forgotten eating my first Early Transparent Gage, a fruit with a basic name that belies the marvel of its taste.

Plums and greengages are susceptible to disease. Aphids can do much damage. Silver leaf affects some varieties, including Victoria, and the fruit can be ruined by Plum Sawfly and Plum Moths. Wasps are a great danger when picking ripe fruit.

On and off, all that hot French August, we made ourselves ill from eating the greengages. Joss and I felt guilty; we were still at the age when we thought being greedy was a childish fault and this gave our guilt a tinge of hopelessness because, up to then, we had believed that as we grew older our faults would disappear, and none of them did.

Rumer Godden,
The Greengage Summer, 1958

Plum Jam

Perhaps the best jam I have ever made was with plums bought at a farm shop on the road back from Wales. They were Victoria plums, under-ripe and fresh. Plums contain enough pectin to make the addition of lemon juice unnecessary. I made jam to the same recipe from the first crop of Opal plums from the allotments a few years later.

2kg net weight of slightly under ripe plums
  halved and stoned
Kernels from the plum stones
1.75kg sugar

Prepare the plums and leave in a big bowl overnight with the sugar. Next day, skin the kernels and add them to the plums. In a preserving pan, slowly heat the jam mixture to boiling point. Let it bubble quite actively until the scum dies down a little and an area of clear surface can be seen. Then it can be left to cook at a steady rate, stirring occasionally to make sure that the plums are not sticking to the bottom of the pan. Test after 20 minutes and, when ready, pour into prepared jam jars and cover.

Plum Gratinée

450g ripe plums
120g caster sugar

3 large egg yolks
375 ml double cream

Prepare the fruit by halving and taking out the stones and arrange either into individual gratin dishes or one large dish. Sprinkle with a little of the sugar and bake for about 20 minutes in a medium oven until the plums begin to soften.

In a bowl, whisk the sugar and egg yolks together until pale and thick. Add the cream and beat for a further two minutes until the mixture thickens slightly. Pour this sabayon mixture over the fruit and grill for about five minutes until golden. The result is plums and the richest custard.

PLUM AND ALMOND TART

❊

A simple enough sweet that is good for autumn entertaining.

250g puff pastry, either bought
   or made (see pages 210-11)
   or 250g sablée pastry
   (see page 214)
500g plums
2 tbsp caster sugar

For the almond paste:
30g unsalted butter, softened
30g caster sugar
1 small egg, beaten
15g plain flour
50g ground almonds
2 tbsp brandy

First make the almond paste. Cream the butter and sugar together in a bowl with a wooden spoon. Gradually add the egg, brandy and flour and ground almonds.

Roll out the pastry and place it on a buttered 21-23cm diameter pie dish. Spread on the almond paste. Halve the plums, remove the stones and cut the plums into wedges. Arrange these neatly on the paste. Scatter over the sugar and bake for 20-25 minutes in an oven preheated to 190°C or until the plums are soft and the pastry is coloured. Put the pie on the floor of the oven for the last few minutes to ensure that the pastry on the bottom of the tart is cooked.

Serve warm or cold.

PLUM CLAFOUTIS

65g plain flour
Pinch of sea salt
100g caster sugar
2 eggs
3 egg yolks
250 ml double cream
2 tbsp armagnac
20g butter, plus extra for greasing
Icing sugar, for dusting
500g plums
1 tbsp toasted flaked almonds

Put the flour, salt and sugar in a food processor and whiz for a few seconds to mix. Add the eggs, egg yolks, cream and armagnac and blend to a smooth batter. Pour the mixture into a jug and cover with cling film.

Brush a large ovenproof gratin dish, about 25cm in diameter, with the softened butter, then dust with a little icing sugar.

Cut the plums in half, remove their stones and pat dry. Melt the butter in a nonstick frying pan. Dredge the plum halves in sugar, then add to the pan, cut-side down. Cook over a high heat until slightly caramelised at the edges. Transfer the plums to the prepared gratin dish, cut-side down.

Give the clafoutis batter a final stir then pour it over the plums in the gratin dish. Scatter over the flaked almonds. Bake for 20-25 minutes at 190°C or until risen and golden brown. Gently press the centre of the clafoutis to check it is set.

Dust with icing sugar and serve warm.

SWEET PICKLED GREENGAGES

This recipe was published in *The Independent* where Mark Hix thanks Charles Campion. Alas, it appeared just as our greengages had finished and so it was almost a year before I had a chance to try it but when I did, it was truly delicious. To date my favourite way of serving it, apart from simply with cheese, has been as a first course with slices of fried halloumi.

2kg greengages, halved and stoned
1 litre white distilled vinegar
500g granulated sugar
Seeds from 20 cardamom pods
2 tbsp green peppercorns
5g mace blades
12 dried red chillies

Pack the greengages into four or five half-litre sterilised Kilner or preserving jars with the spices shared equally. Boil the vinegar and sugar for a few minutes, stirring occasionally to be sure the sugar has dissolved. Pour the hot liquid into the jars, close the lids tightly and then turn the jars upside down for 15 minutes or so to seal the liquids. Turn them back up, leave to cool and store in a cool place for up to six months.

POTATOES

Potato was one of the few original illustrations in Gerard's Herball (1597). Gerard wrote that the potato 'roots' he had received from Virginia *'grow & prosper in my garden as in their owne native country'.'Boiled and eaten with oile, vinegar, and pepper or dressed some other way by the hand of a skilfull Cooke'* was his sound advice.

The whole process of growing potatoes is exciting. Watching them chit, preparing the trenches, putting them in and looking out for the first signs of life, then what seems an age before teasing the first of the new potatoes from the ground.

My First Early favourite is Foremost which is large and does not disintegrate while cooking and has a great flavour. Charlotte is another variety that I like to grow. In a third row I plant salad potatoes, either Pink Fir Apple or Ratte. This year space has also been made to plant Roseval. Lots of nostalgia is tied up with varieties of potatoes. Sharpe's Express, Arran Pilot, Homeguard all have a loyal following. It is wise to choose varieties that will spread the crop over several months, a First Early, followed by a Second Early and then a main crop. Blight and disease can strike potatoes. It would be as well to get advice from neighbouring allotment holders about which varieties do well.

Everyday New Potatoes

It is best to steam new potatoes unless you are confident they will not break up. However you cook them, they do need to be watched carefully. I am not sure there is any true advantage in putting potatoes into boiling water rather than cold and perhaps the best advice is to know your potato. Butter, salt and black pepper, with chives, mint or parsley are the only other requirements.

Peas and Beans and New Potatoes

This is a recipe using ingredients that only come together late in July and oozes with the taste of summer freshness.

Cook some new potatoes in salted water at the bottom of a steamer with peas and small broad beans in the steamer above. When cooked, stir them into a rich béchamel sauce (see p. 213). Delicious served with grilled chicken.

Cumin Potatoes

3 tbsp olive oil
3 cm piece of root ginger,
  coarsely grated
4 cloves garlic, chopped
1 red chilli, medium heat

1 tsp ground turmeric
1 tbsp cumin seeds, crushed
750g new potatoes, scrubbed
Salt and freshly ground
  black pepper

Heat the oil in a saucepan with a lid, add the ginger, garlic, and chilli and cook gently for two minutes. Add the remaining spices and let the cumin 'pop'. Put the potatoes in the pan and stir to cover them with the sauce, then pour in about 100ml of water. Bring to the boil, cover and cook for about 20 minutes, checking the water from time to time until the potatoes are cooked and resting in a thick sauce. Season and serve immediately.

POMMES LYONNAISE

This is an exquisite dish in which to use larger new potatoes. It is important that the two elements should be cooked separately.

1kg potatoes
2 tbsp finely chopped shallots
125g butter
Salt and freshly ground black pepper

Boil the potatoes in their skins, then drain them and when cool enough to handle, skin them and cut into slices, preferably using a mandoline. Fry the slices gently in large heavy bottomed frying pan, using most of the butter, until browned on both sides.

When the potatoes begin to colour, in a separate pan, fry the shallots in the remaining butter until they too colour. When both pans are ready, pour the shallots over the potatoes, season, and serve.

POMMES LYONNAISE PLUS...

The above dish can be made more substantial by mixing slices of hard-boiled egg with potatoes that have simply been boiled, skinned, and sliced, but not sautéed. Cook the shallots as above but increase the heat for the last moments of cooking and add, first, a handful of chopped parsley and, then, a few drops of white wine vinegar before pouring over the potatoes and eggs. Serve warm.

Potato Salad with a Vinaigrette Dressing

Waxy salad potatoes that have been steamed or boiled in salted water, then skinned, sliced, and mixed while still warm with a salad dressing made from 2:1 olive oil to white wine vinegar, salt, pepper and a hint of garlic. Decorate with chopped chives.

Potato Salad with a Mayonnaise Dressing

Prepare the potatoes as in the preceding recipe. The sauce is made from homemade mayonnaise (see page 212) thinned a little with milk to which salt, black pepper, and chopped chives have been added. Chopped parsley and mint can be sprinkled on top.

Baked New Potatoes with Sour Cream and Caviar

20 new potatoes
40g crème fraîche
30g caviar
Finely chopped chives

Baked new potatoes are fun. Cook the potatoes in an oven heated to 200°C for about 40 minutes or until soft when tested with a skewer. Remove and allow to cool a little. Cut a cross at the top of each potato, put a spoonful of the crème fraîche inside and top with a little caviar. Decorate with the chopped chives.

HOMITY PIE

A simple dish which gives centre stage to potatoes. If possible, use waxy potatoes such as Ratte or Charlotte.

200g rich short crust pastry
 (see page 214)
675g potatoes, unpeeled
2 medium onions
A few drops olive oil

4 cloves garlic
175g Cheddar cheese, grated
4 tbsp chopped flat leaf parsley
Salt and freshly ground black
 pepper

Line a 20cm flan dish with the pastry and bake blind for 10 minutes. Cover the potatoes with cold water, bring to the boil and simmer for 10-15 minutes until almost cooked. Drain and set aside. Meanwhile, chop the onions, crush the garlic and cook very gently in the oil until translucent. Thinly slice the potatoes. Place into a large bowl and mix together with onions and garlic, parsley and half of the cheese. Season well. Put this mixture loosely into the pastry case. Top with the remaining cheese and cook for 20-25 minutes at 190°C. Good hot or cold.

RÖSTI WITH SMOKED SALMON AND WATERCRESS

There is a lot of polemic connected with rösti, the famous dish of German-speaking Switzerland. My recipe is inspired by Donna Hay from her book *New Fast Food* and ignores all the pitfalls and politics. Waxy potatoes, such as Charlotte, work well. Salmon is the obvious topping but scrambled eggs and bacon would be just as good.

Take two large potatoes and grate them into a bowl with two tablespoons of melted butter and one of chopped dill or parsley. Warm a little sunflower oil in a frying pan and fry flattened spoonfuls of the potato mixture in batches, cooking them on each side until crisp and golden. Drain on kitchen paper.

Serve as 'burgers' with watercress (or rocket) lightly placed between two rösti, then add the crème fraîche and top with smoked salmon.

Jansson's Temptation

I love this dish which is the perfect meal for a late evening supper. It is essential to use anchovies in brine and not oil and even better to use Swedish tinned anchovies which are sweet and mild. To use crème fraîche may seem extravagant but, for me, it gives a hint of acidity without taking away from the richness of the dish.

1 large onion, peeled and finely chopped
500g potatoes, cut into slices, preferably using a mandoline, or 'chipped'
1 small tin anchovy fillets in brine or Swedish Abba brand anchovies
100 ml double cream
200 ml crème fraîche
Salt and freshly ground white pepper
1 slice brown bread, crusts removed,
    toasted and made into breadcrumbs
100g butter

Fry the onion gently in half of the butter until translucent and soft. Place the prepared potato slices in cold water to reduce starch content and prevent them turning brown. Strain and chop the anchovy fillets but retain the liquid. Mix the anchovy liquid with the cream and crème fraîche. Season with a little white pepper and possibly salt, depending on the strength of the brine.

In a shallow gratin dish layer the potatoes, onions, and anchovies, starting and finishing with potatoes. Carefully spoon over the cream sauce and sprinkle over the breadcrumbs. Dot on the remaining butter. Bake at 200°C for 45–50 minutes or until the potatoes are cooked and the top nicely browned.

Serve with cucumber, dill, and gherkins, or a green salad.

PUMPKINS AND SQUASHES

Late October and pumpkins are synonymous with Halloween. Even small pumpkins are too much for one meal but can be kept wrapped in the fridge for up to a week and served in different guises. Roasting suits pumpkins well. Even more than with potatoes or tomatoes, we bow to the American heritage of pumpkins and squashes and turn to the US for many recipes.

"Each year, the Great Pumpkin rises out of the pumpkin patch that he thinks is the most sincere. He's gotta pick this one. He's got to. I don't see how a pumpkin patch can be more sincere than this one. You can look around and there's not a sign of hypocrisy. Nothing but sincerity as far as the eye can see."

Charles M Schulz, *It's the Great Pumpkin, Charlie Brown*,
Animated TV special 1966,
directed by Bill Melendez.

PUMPKIN AND GINGER SOUP

I love pumpkin soups for their silkiness. There are endless variations on pumpkin soup but this is my favourite.

1 small leek, roughly chopped
1 small onion, peeled and chopped
A large knob of butter
30g root ginger, scraped and finely chopped
A few sprigs of thyme
½ tsp crushed chilli flakes
1kg pumpkin or butternut squash, peeled, seeded and roughly chopped
1.5 litres vegetable stock
Salt and freshly ground black pepper

Gently cook the leek, onion, ginger and thyme in the butter until soft. Add the crushed chillies, pumpkin, and the vegetable stock. Bring to the boil, season and simmer for 20 minutes.

When all the vegetables are cooked, blend the soup in batches in a liquidiser until smooth and then strain through a sieve. Reheat, check seasoning and serve in bowls with a spoonful of plain yoghurt or soured cream on the top of each portion.

EVERYDAY ROASTED PUMPKIN OR SQUASH

Cut a pumpkin or squash in two. Take out the seeds (pumpkin seeds can be kept for roasting, see next page), and clean away the fibrous strands. Cut into large chunks and then into cubes. Lastly, take off the skin. Put into a baking dish. Sprinkle with a little olive oil and season. Mix well so that all sides of the pumpkin are coated. Roast for about 40 minutes at 190°C. Oregano, chilli flakes or sage could be added to give flavour.

Pumpkins and squashes can be mixed with other autumn vegetables such as parsnips, sweet potatoes, beetroot and carrots to make a comforting dish of assorted roasted vegetables.

ROASTED PUMPKIN SEEDS

Pumpkin seeds, arduously cleaned of the fibrous flesh, washed and dried, can be roasted spread out on a large baking sheet. They can be dry roasted (with or without salt), or roasted in a little olive oil and salt. Either way, roast them in a hot oven (200°C) for about 10-15 minutes until lightly browned. Check the progress of the seeds frequently and move them around the tin to ensure even colouring.

The fibrous husk of the seeds can be made more digestible by simmering the prepared seeds in lightly salted water for 10 minutes. Then drain them, spread the seeds out on kitchen paper to dry before lightly coating them in olive oil with a little salt and roasting as above.

PUMPKIN WITH RACLETTE

The idea of having pumpkin cubes as well as potatoes to serve with raclette came from a recipe in Jill Dupleix's *Very Simple Food*. Without a raclette machine, put cubes of cooked pumpkin and potato on a baking tray and top with slices of raclette or other sliced cheeses such as Gruyère which melt easily. Bake in a hot oven for a few minutes until the cheese is soft and bubbling. Leaves of oregano, sage or thyme on top of the cheese would give extra flavour.

Serve with cold smoked meats accompanied with pickled gherkins and cocktail onions.

ROAST PUMPKIN RISOTTO

This recipe is a variation on one in Donna Hay's *New Fast Food*. The saltiness of the Feta is a good contrast to the sweetness of the pumpkin. A little sumac sprinkled on at the end gives a citrus note.

300g pumpkin, peeled, deseeded and cut into small chunks
Olive oil
300g Arborio rice
Chicken stock
1 medium onion, skinned and thinly sliced
Salt and freshly ground black pepper
Parmesan cheese
125g Feta cheese
Stoned black olives
½ tsp chilli flakes
Chopped chives
Sumac (optional)

Place the pumpkin on a baking tray and toss with olive oil, salt, pepper, and the chilli flakes. Roast in a hot oven for 20 minutes or until soft.

In a large frying pan, gently sauté the onion in a little olive oil. When soft but not coloured, add the rice and stir it around for a minute or two before adding a little of the stock. Keep adding stock for about 20 minutes as it is absorbed by the rice until the rice is almost cooked. Care should now be taken to add only enough stock so that the rice is moist but not sodden. Add the pumpkin and check the seasoning. Stir in the Parmesan cheese and a handful of stoned black olives. Decorate with broken pieces of Feta cheese, chopped chives and, optionally, some sumac sprinkled on top, before serving.

RASPBERRIES

I never remember a time without raspberries or there being home-made raspberry jam. A bowl of raspberries with cream and sugar is perfection. Richard Olney in *Simple French Food* agrees. For him perfection plus would be the addition of fresh, peeled almonds, some whipped cream diluted with raspberry purée – though he admits this may interfere with the appreciation of the accompanying Sauternes. Raspberries, cream, sugar, and Sauterne: I can truly think of no dessert more exquisite.

Just picking ripe raspberries from the cane is a sublime moment. By growing both summer and autumn raspberries, their season can be extended. Raspberries are a northern European fruit and the names of many favourite varieties, such as Glen Ample and Glen Moy bear traces of their Scottish ancestry. Yellow varieties, such as Allgold give novelty as do the purple Glen Coe.

Rasberries can be frozen. I usually gently cook any raspberries to be frozen but they can be put straight into the freezer.

RASPBERRIES AND ZABAGLIONE

300g raspberries
2 large egg yolks
4 tbsp Marsala
2 tsp caster sugar

To make the zabaglione, put the egg yolks,
Marsala and sugar in a bowl and place it over a pan
of gently simmering water. Whisk for two minutes or until
the mixture is thick and frothy and then remove from the heat.

Arrange the raspberries on serving plates and pour over the
zabaglione.

RASPBERRY AND ALMOND EVE'S PUDDING

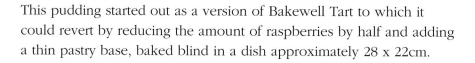

This pudding started out as a version of Bakewell Tart to which it
could revert by reducing the amount of raspberries by half and adding
a thin pastry base, baked blind in a dish approximately 28 x 22cm.

400g fresh raspberries
100g granulated sugar.
100g unsalted butter
125g caster sugar
3 large eggs, separated
150g ground almonds

Gently cook the raspberries and the granulated sugar
until the juices run. Turn into a pie dish.

To make the topping, beat together the butter and caster sugar
until light and fluffy. Gradually add the egg yolks and ground almonds.
Whisk the egg whites until stiff and gently fold these into the mixture.
Spoon the mixture over the raspberries and cook at 180°C for about
30 minutes or until the top is golden and springy. Sprinkle over
some caster sugar. Serve while still warm with cream.

HOT RASPBERRY SOUFFLÉS

❦

250g raspberries
100g icing sugar
Juice of ½ lemon
2 egg yolks
8 egg whites
Scant pinch of salt
Softened butter and a sprinkling of caster sugar to coat soufflé dishes
A little icing sugar

Liquidise the raspberries with half of the icing sugar, lemon juice and egg yolks until smooth. Sieve into a bowl. Smear generously the insides of four individual soufflé dishes with softened butter and sprinkle on caster sugar to stick to the butter. Excess sugar can be moved from one dish onto the next.

Whisk the egg whites with the salt until soft and snowy. Continue whisking, adding by degrees the remaining icing sugar until the mixture starts to look glossy. Whisk about a quarter of the egg whites into the raspberry mixture to loosen it and then fold in the rest with a metal spoon. Fill the dishes to the rim and then smooth the surface with a pallet knife.

Put the soufflés on a flat metal tray and bake for about 12-15 minutes at 220°C. For a nicely crusted surface, remove the soufflés after they have been in the oven for a few minutes, sift over a little icing sugar and return to the oven.

Serve with cream.

Pavlova with Raspberries

Red currants, blackberries or mixed fruit could also be used. Thick fruit purée could be added, mixed with the cream or poured over to give a ripple effect.

For the meringue:
3 egg whites
100g caster sugar
1 tsp corn flour
1 tsp white wine vinegar
A few drops of vanilla essence

200 ml double cream
1 tbsp caster sugar
250g raspberries

To make the meringue, in a clean bowl whisk the egg whites until stiff, slowly add the caster sugar a spoonful at a time and continue whisking until the mixture is stiff and shiny. Add the corn flour and vinegar and whisk again for a few seconds. Spoon the mixture onto a baking tray lined with silicone, to form a round shape, slightly depressed in the centre.

Cook in an oven set at a low temperature (110°C) for 1½ hours or longer. Remove from the oven and allow to cool.

Whip the cream with the sugar. Put onto the pavlova base and scatter over the berries. Serve immediately.

RASPBERRY MOUSSE

I am not sure if this is a mousse or a soufflé but it is certainly a favourite and works just as well with damsons or blackberries.

400g raspberries
100g caster sugar
450 ml double cream
1 large tbsp gelatine
4 egg whites

In a food processor, blend the raspberries and sugar to a purée and then sieve. Prepare the gelatine as instructed and add to the raspberries.

Whip the cream to soft peaks and add the raspberry mixture and lastly whisk the egg whites until stiff and fold these in. Turn the mousse into a bowl or four ramekin dishes and put in the fridge until set.

RASPBERRY COULIS

Raspberries Liquidised with half their weight of icing sugar and sieved make a perfect coulis and become an essential ingredient in a peach Melba.

UNBOILED RASPBERRY JAM

This excellent recipe came from my allotment neighbour Louise Pavey.

Equal weights of raspberries and fine white sugar

Put the raspberries and sugar into separate large dishes which will fit into the oven. Let them get very hot but not boiling (this takes 20-30 minutes at a medium temperature). Remove from oven and turn sugar and fruit into a large bowl (warmed) and mix them thoroughly together with a wooden spoon. Turn at once into jars and seal down.

This jam will keep for a year.

RASPBERRY RIPPLE ICE CREAM

This ice cream is made over a day. Each step is easy and the result is seriously rewarding.

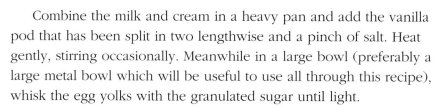

400 ml whole milk
200 ml double cream
1 vanilla pod
Pinch of salt
6 egg yolks
120g granulated sugar
400g raspberries
150g caster sugar

Combine the milk and cream in a heavy pan and add the vanilla pod that has been split in two lengthwise and a pinch of salt. Heat gently, stirring occasionally. Meanwhile in a large bowl (preferably a large metal bowl which will be useful to use all through this recipe), whisk the egg yolks with the granulated sugar until light.

When the milk is hot but not boiling, remove it from the heat and stir it into the egg mixture. Continuing to stir, pour it back into the saucepan or a double saucepan and, on a very low heat and using a whisk, beat the mixture while it thickens. Remove from the heat and immediately cool the mixture by placing the pan in cold water. I find it best to have a sink prepared with a suitable depth of water. When cool, cover with cling film and chill it in the fridge for at least an hour.

Now comes the exciting part. Sieve the custard mixture to remove the vanilla pod and seeds and be sure there are no lumps, pour it into an ice cream maker and churn for about 30 minutes or until it begins to set.

Blend the raspberries with the sugar and sieve to make a syrup.

To make the ripple, spoon the ice cream into a very cold bowl and fold in the raspberry syrup. Spoon into an ice cream container and freeze.

Remove from the deep freeze and place in the fridge 20 minutes before use.

Raspberry Flummery

150 ml full fat milk

A small piece of lemon peel

2 tbsp caster sugar

1 tbsp semolina

100g raspberries

3 egg whites

For the custard:

60 ml full fat milk

50 ml double cream

A few drops of vanilla essence

3 egg yolks

1 tbsp caster sugar

1 tsp cornflour

Bring the milk to the boil with the lemon peel and 1 tablespoon of the sugar, then whisk in the semolina and cook on a low heat for 3-4 minutes, stirring constantly. Leave to cool.

To make the custard, slowly bring the milk and cream almost to the boil with the vanilla essence. In a bowl, whisk together the egg yolks, caster sugar and cornflour, then pour on the milk and cream and continue whisking. Return the mixture to the pan and stir over a low heat for a few minutes until it thickens. Transfer to a clean bowl and place cling film over the bowl to prevent a skin forming.

Whisk the egg whites until stiff, add remaining tablespoon of sugar and continue to whisk for a couple of minutes until the mixture shines. Gently fold in the semolina mixture and then add the raspberries. Pour into glasses and add custard before serving.

CRANACHAN

❧

I love this pudding which is the only one to have on Burns Night or to celebrate St Andrew. I like to combine a few gently cooked raspberries with fresh ones. This is different but equally delicious made with rhubarb.

60g porridge oats	4 tbsp Drambuie or whisky
600 ml double cream	200g raspberries
4 tbsp honey	2 tbsp caster sugar

    Lightly cook half the raspberries with the sugar and allow to cool. Spread the oats onto a baking tray and toast in a medium oven until golden. Check them closely as they turn colour quickly. Whisk the cream until stiff, and then stir in the honey, Drambuie (or whisky) and most of the oats.

    Using four individual dishes or glasses, place the cooked raspberries on the bottom, add the cream mixture and then top with the fresh raspberries and the remaining oats.

RASPBERRY VINEGAR

❧

A few drops from a bottle of raspberry vinegar can give an instant lift to lamb chops, salad dressing and is a revelation when served with vanilla ice cream.

450g raspberries
450 ml white wine vinegar
80g granulated sugar

    Put the raspberries in a bowl and crush them gently with a fork. Add the vinegar and stir. Cover with clingfilm and leave for two days, stirring occasionally.

    Drain through muslin. Bring the liquid with the sugar to the boil slowly in a stainless steel pan. Let it simmer for 10 minutes.

    When cool, store in sterilized bottles.

RHUBARB

No one is indifferent to rhubarb. Jane Grigson admits to disliking it but I am grateful to her for one of my favourite recipes, Rhubarb and Grapefruit Jam. Rhubarb needs careful attention. Use only the young, fresh stalks. Traditional flavourings for rhubarb are orange or ginger but a few leaves of sweet Cicely added while the rhubarb cooks give it a sweetness and mild aniseed flavour. Vanilla is an excellent flavouring for cold rhubarb. Blood oranges, which are in the shops around Easter, are especially good and, towards the end of the rhubarb season, strawberries can give a new dimension to its taste.

The Chinese for rhubarb, 大黃 (da huang), translates as big yellow and refers to its root. The root, used extensively in traditional Chinese medicine, was one of the important exports from China to the west in the fifteenth century. Gradually rhubarb was grown along the Silk Route and especially cultivated on banks of the Volga River. It was not grown in England until the seventeenth century.

Rhubarb is the first edible sign of spring on the allotment. Early rhubarb can be forced through a chimney pot but pickings truly start late in March and continue until early July.

Rhubarb has a high water content and the secret to many of these recipes is to avoid too much liquid. In any recipe in which the rhubarb is first gently cooked, excess liquid can always be strained off, sweetened, and reduced to form a syrup or made into a jelly. A measure of Campari or grenadine could be added to give extra interest.

RHUBARB ICE CREAM

750g prepared rhubarb, cut into pieces
300g granulated sugar
300ml single cream
300ml double cream
3 egg yolks
50g caster sugar
Seeds from a vanilla pod (optional)

Put the rhubarb into a dish with the sugar.
Cover with tin foil and bake at 190° C for about
35 minutes or until soft and cooked. Cool and
strain (keeping the liquid to make a syrup or
jelly). Using a blender beat the pulp until it is
smooth. Leave to cool.

Heat the single cream (with the vanilla seeds if using) slowly until
almost boiling and pour it over the egg yolks and the caster sugar.
Using a double pan simmer the custard slowly, stirring constantly
with a wooden spoon for about 10 minutes until the custard thickens.
Remove it immediately from the heat and cool the custard as quickly
as possible by pouring it into a large bowl and immersing the bowl in
cold water in the sink.

When the custard is cool, stir in the rhubarb pulp. Whip the double
cream until stiff and stir this into the fruit custard.

Turn into the ice-cream maker to freeze.

RHUBARB CRUMBLE

Probably the best of all crumbles. The same topping can be used for apples or plums though you may prefer to the substitute cinnamon for ginger. A gooseberry crumble flavoured with elderflowers is excellent.

350g prepared rhubarb
60g demerara sugar
60g butter
60g caster or soft brown sugar
60g plain flour
30g porridge oats
60g ground almonds
1 tsp ground ginger

Cut the rhubarb into lengths of 2 cm. Put it into a baking dish and sprinkle over the demerara sugar. Bake for 10 minutes at 180°C to allow the rhubarb to cook slightly. Allow to cool a little.

Meanwhile mix together all the other ingredients with your fingers. The crumble mixture does not need to be too fine. Turn the mixture over the rhubarb and 'arrange' it gently with a fork. Bake at 180°C for 25-30 minutes or until the surface is light brown with some darker brown blisters.

Serve warm with cream or custard.

RHUBARB AND ORANGE CAKE

This recipe is a great favourite.

400g rhubarb, trimmed and cut into 2cm pieces
200g golden caster sugar
150g butter, softened
2 eggs lightly beaten
75g self-raising flour
½ tsp baking powder
100g ground almonds
Grated zest of 1 small orange
2 tbsp orange juice
25g flaked almonds

Grease a round 21cm springform cake tin and line its base with baking parchment. Place the rhubarb in a bowl and cover with 50g of the sugar. Leave for 30 minutes while you prepare the rest of the cake.

Beat together the remaining sugar and the butter, then whisk in the eggs. Using a metal spoon gently fold in the flour, baking powder and ground almonds and then the orange zest and juice.

Stir the rhubarb and its sugary juices into the cake mixture and spoon into the prepared tin. Place on a baking tray, sprinkle over the almond flakes and bake for 25 minutes at 190°C. Reduce the temperature to 180°C and cook for a further 20-25 minutes, or until the cake is firm to the touch. Allow to cool in the tin for 10 minutes before taking out.

Serve warm or cold with whipped cream.

Rhubarb and Grapefruit Jam

A recipe adapted from Jane Grigson's *Fruit Book*.

750g prepared rhubarb, cut into 2cm lengths
2 or 3 grapefruit
750g sugar

Put the rhubarb in a large bowl, removing any stringy lengths. Grate or zest the grapefruit. Remove the pith from the grapefruit and Liquidise the flesh and then press it through a sieve. Add zest and sieved grapefruit liquid to the rhubarb. Pour over the sugar and leave overnight.

The next day, in a heavy pan bring the jam mixture slowly to the boil, stirring often. When the sugar has completely dissolved, raise the heat and boil hard for 20 minutes or until set.

Test to see if setting point is reached. It will not be a firm setting jam. Pot as usual. Enough for three ½ kg (1lb) jars

Mark Hix's Ricotta with Spiced Rhubarb

250-300g rhubarb, trimmed and cut into 1cm chunks
150g granulated sugar
2 tbsp ginger liqueur or ginger syrup
A good pinch of dried chilli flakes
2 tsp grenadine
250-300g Ricotta at room temperature

Put the sugar, ginger, chilli and grenadine into a saucepan with 200ml water, bring to the boil and allow to simmer for a few minutes. Stir in the rhubarb, cover and barely simmer until the rhubarb is just cooked.

To serve, spoon the Ricotta on to serving plates and place the rhubarb and syrup around.

RHUBARB CORDIAL

This should make enough cordial for one large bottle. Flavours can be introduced. Adding one star anise when cooking the rhubarb would give the cordial a mild aniseed flavour. A few rose petals cooked with the rhubarb and a tablespoon of rosewater added before bottling give a hint of 'Turkish Delight'.

450g prepared rhubarb, cut into short lengths
350g granulated sugar
1 tsp citric acid

Cook the rhubarb and sugar in a large heavy saucepan with enough water to cover the fruit for 20 minutes or until the fruit is pulpy.

When cool, strain the liquid through muslin, pressing the pulp to extract all the juice.

Return the juice to the pan and bring to the boil. Take off the heat and add the citric acid.

Store immediately in warmed, sterilized bottles. The syrup will keep for up to a month in the refrigerator.

SPINACH

pinach grew first in Iran and neighbouring countries. By the seventh century, it had been carried to China by Arab traders. The Chinese for 'spinach', bo cai, 菠菜, is a derivation of 'Persian vegetable'.

By growing different sorts of spinach, there are few months of the year when it cannot be found on the allotment and, if none is available, Swiss chard can make a good substitute. Snails lurk among spinach leaves and it is wise to take time to wash it well in salted water.

Eggs, butter, cheese, and garlic are ideal companions with nutmeg a complementary spice.

'There is scarcely any limit to the amount of butter which spinach will absorb'.

Elizabeth David,
French Provincial Cooking, 1960.

Everyday Spinach

Wash the spinach and take off any of the tougher stalks. Drain well. You may choose to chop up the spinach leaves or leave them whole. Melt a generous knob or two of butter in a heavy-bottomed pan. Add the spinach; there will be enough water still on the leaves to not need more and stir around in the butter with a wooden spoon until the spinach shrinks. A little salt and crushed garlic can be added towards the end of cooking.

Left-overs can be kept for use in a frittata or omelette.

Épinards en Purée

Spinach cooked in a little water can be drained, squeezed dry and very finely chopped. Returned to a thick-bottomed saucepan on a very low heat with a good amount of butter it is transformed into Épinards en Purée, a delicious sauce for escalopes.

Chinese Spinach

A bunch of young spinach, washed
2 cloves garlic, crushed
2 tbsp corn oil
1 or 2 red chillies finely chopped
Scant handful of peanuts

Preheat a wok. Add two tablespoons of oil and, when hot, add the garlic, followed in reasonable haste by the spinach and chillies. It will take only a few minutes for the spinach to shrink. Serve topped with peanuts.

Oriental Spinach Salad

Tender young spinach leaves are well served by this recipe. The vegetables and the amount used are optional but it is fun to experiment and give variety of taste and texture. A light lunch can be made from this salad by adding chunks of tofu, fried or plain.

2 red peppers
Baby leaf spinach
A selection of pea sprouts and young salad leaves
Spring onions

For the dressing:
2 tbsp olive oil
2 tbsp orange juice
2 tbsp balsamic vinegar
2 tbsp light soya sauce
1 red chilli, deseeded and very
    finely chopped
½ red onion very finely chopped
A little freshly ground black pepper
A few pomegranate seeds to decorate (optional)

Skin the peppers by placing them under a hot grill, turning them until they are black on all sides. When cool enough to handle, strip off the skins, halve and deseed the peppers. Cut them into strips.

Clean the spring onions and remove tops. Cut them into diagonal strips about 2 cm in length. Wash the spinach, remove any stalks and shred the leaves. Wash all the other salad ingredients and add to the spinach. Dry well before arranging in a bowl and adding the peppers and spring onion on top.

Mix all the dressing ingredients and spoon half over the salad. Finally, decorate with pomegranate seeds. Serve with extra dressing on the side.

Any spare dressing can be kept in a closed jam jar in the fridge for up to a week.

WILTED SPINACH WITH CANNELLINI BEANS AND TOMATOES

A good mid-week dish.

6 tomatoes

A large bunch of spinach, washed and with the tougher stalks removed

4-5 tbsp olive oil

½ red onion, finely chopped

Salt and freshly ground black pepper

3 cloves garlic, very finely chopped

A few crushed chillies

2 tins cannellini beans (or dried beans that have been prepared)

1 large handful parsley, finely chopped

Cut the tops off the tomatoes and put them flat side down with a little of the oil in a large deep frying pan with a lid. Cook gently in a the covered pan for about 15 minutes. The juice will start to run and the skin come away from the flesh. Remove the skin as it loosens and then cook the tomatoes a little more, with the lid not tight, until they are soft and the sauce thickens. Put to one side.

Again, in a large frying pan, using most of the remaining oil, fry the onion gently for five minutes. Add crushed chillies, cannellini beans and cook for another few minutes. Add the garlic. Wilt the spinach in a little boiling water. Drain well and mix in the remaining oil. Add spinach, tomatoes and parsley to the bean mixture and, when heated through, serve.

To make this dish more substantial, cheese, such as Feta or Ricotta, could be crumbled over the top before serving.

STRAWBERRIES

'*A* strawberry that becomes acquainted with water loses its virtue' wrote Jane Grigson. I would go further and add that they should never be picked until a day after rain. The old fashioned way of putting straw around plants does help keep fruit dry and clean but mats, either bought or made from thick plastic, also work well.

Our old strawberry beds are of Cambridge Late Pine, Florence, and Gariguette. For years they did well and, with exception of Florence, the aim of having a three year cycle using runners to create a new row each year was successful. Now they are untidy and it is best to start again in a new site with well-prepared soil. I will keep a row of wood strawberries that was fashioned from plants that strayed from a neighbouring plot but, in the new bed, will plant Mara Des Bois and Cambridge. A variety that is very impressive on a neighbouring plot is Honeoye. It has proved both heavy cropping and flavoursome.

Hulled strawberries or a purée made from strawberries and icing sugar can be served with vanilla ice cream (see page 220), pannacotta (see pages 216-17), cheesecake (see page 218), pavlova (see page 174), in a chocolate roulade (see page 221) or purée can be used to make a mousse, soufflés and any number of other puddings. Soft cream cheese and strawberry purée is a delicacy at the end of a meal.

When I was last in Holborn,
I saw good strawberries in your garden there
I do beseech you send for some of them.

Gloucester

Richard III, Act 3, scene 4

MELON AND PARMA HAM WITH STRAWBERRY SALSA

This is David Cheadle's recipe which is a great favourite at the French class summer party. It is a stunning first course.

1 large ripe melon (Canteloupe, Charentais or Galia)
300g Parma or Serrano ham, thinly sliced

For the salsa:
500g strawberries
1 tsp caster sugar
1 tbsp groundnut or sunflower oil
1 tbsp orange juice
½ tsp of finely grated orange rind
½ tsp of finely grated fresh root ginger
Salt and freshly ground black pepper

Halve the melon and scoop out seeds, cut into slices with or without the rind.

Prepare the salsa by hulling the strawberries and dicing them. Place them in a mixing bowl with the sugar and crush lightly to release juices. Add the other ingredients and season with salt and plenty of black pepper.

Arrange the melon and ham on individual plates and spoon over the salsa.

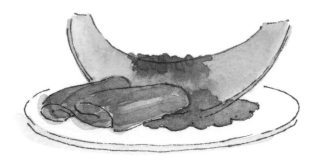

OLD FASHIONED STRAWBERRY SHORTCAKE

Nothing to do with the kitschy cartoon character that first appeared on American greetings cards in the 1970s before blossoming into dolls, stickers and even a musical, these biscuits are like double scones that need to be eaten as soon as they are ready. For a one-off tea time treat, I like to make this as one big shortcake to be served in slices.

600g strawberries
100g caster sugar
500 ml double cream

For the shortcake:
500g plain flour
100g caster sugar
Good pinch of salt
5 level tsps baking powder
300g butter
250 ml single cream

Set aside the best berries for decoration. Quarter the rest and sprinkle them with the sugar. Whip the cream until thick but still pourable. Keep strawberries and cream in the fridge.

To make the shortcake, sift together the dry ingredients and rub in 200g of the butter. Mix to a soft dough with the cream (you may not need all the cream allowed). Knead the dough for a minute, then roll it out to about .75 cm thickness. Cut out two circles about 22 cm diameter or 12 circles about 7cm diameter. Place the one large or six smaller circles on a baking sheet that has been lined with baking paper and greased with butter. Paint a little softened butter on the top of the rounds and place the remaining circle(s) on top.

Bake in a hot oven (220°C). Check after 10 minutes and turn the tray. Leave cooking for about another five minutes or until the rounds are golden brown. The single cake will take a little longer to cook.

When cool enough to handle, pull the two sides apart. Spread the inner sides with the last of the butter and top one side with the sugared berries. Put the second circle on top of the first, inner side upmost and decorate with the whole strawberries. Serve with the whipped cream.

HOT STRAWBERRY SOUFFLÉ

This recipe, from Elizabeth David's *Summer Cooking*, in a way started this book. I came across it and it gave me the solution of what to do with too many, not the most attractive strawberries.

250g strawberries, pulped
3 eggs
60g dried breadcrumbs
200g sugar

Sieve the strawberries. Cream together the yolks of the eggs and the sugar, add to the strawberry pulp and then add the breadcrumbs. Fold in the stiffly beaten whites of the eggs. Turn into a sugared soufflé dish and steam, uncovered, on top of the stove for about 45 minutes. For the last ten minutes move the dish into a slow oven so that the soufflé turns a pale biscuit colour on the top.

This does not turn out like an ordinary soufflé, but has a very spongey consistency. Ground almonds can be substituted for some of the breadcrumbs.

Ricotta al Forno with Strawberries and Marsala

An Italian alternative to baked custard.

A little sunflower oil for greasing
750g Ricotta
100 ml double cream
A few drops vanilla extract
2 medium eggs, plus 1 egg yolk
150g icing sugar, sifted
800g strawberries
100 ml Marsala
150g caster sugar, or less

Line a large loaf tin with foil and brush lightly with oil. Beat the Ricotta with the cream until smooth. Beat in the vanilla, eggs and egg yolk, and then work in the icing sugar. Spoon into the tin and smooth down. Cover with oiled foil. Stand the loaf tin in a roasting tin. Bake for one hour at 170°C, then remove the foil from the top and bake for a further 15-30 minutes until just firm and golden brown.

Leave to cool, then cover and chill.

Hull and halve the strawberries. Mix with the Marsala and icing sugar. Leave to stand for about an hour.

Serve in slices with the strawberries spooned over.

SWEDES

A vegetable of northern Europe, swedes were known to have been growing in Sweden in the early 17th century. In Scandinavia there is a great tradition of serving swedes. Finland has 'lanttulaatikko', where swede is mashed then baked with breadcrumbs and spices. In Sweden 'rotmos', mashed swede with potato or carrot or both, is very popular in winter and usually served with smoked pork. In Scotland, where swedes grow well, there is 'clapshot', mashed swede with potatoes and chives. Wales has its national dish, 'cawl'; a winter soup.

There are many different names for Swede which, confusingly, is also known as yellow turnip or white turnip. In France and North America, swedes are called rutabaga, from the Swedish 'rotabagge', meaning ram root. The normal name in Sweden today is 'kåirot', meaning cabbage or kale root. Even in Scotland, the swede has many names but it is 'neeps' that are always served with haggis.

Like turnips, the freshest leaves from swedes can be cooked. I like them best with onion and a little chilli.

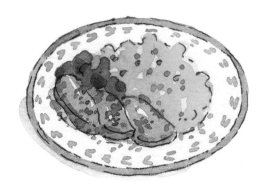

Everyday Swedes

Peel the swedes and cut them into small chunks. Cook until soft, then mash with a potato masher and add butter and plenty of freshly ground black pepper. Mashed potatoes or mashed carrots, cooked separately, can also be added. Finely chopped parsley can be stirred in or sprinkled over the top.

Casserole of Winter Vegetables

This is a great dish to serve in the centre of the table to accompany the Sunday roast. The vegetables given below can be varied. Potatoes could be included and leeks too (though these are best put in together with the stock and not fried). By cutting the vegetables in different ways, the dish is made more of a medley.

A medium sized swede, peeled and cut into 1 cm cubes
4 carrots, peeled and cut at an angle into 1 cm lengths
2 parsnips, peeled and quartered lengthwise
2 turnips, peeled and cut into sections
10 shallots, peeled but left whole
4 cloves of garlic, peeled
1 tbsp olive oil
100g butter
Salt and freshly ground black pepper
3 sprigs of rosemary
100 ml vegetable stock

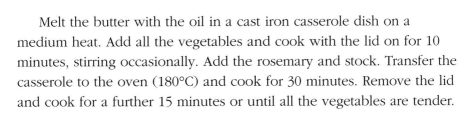

Melt the butter with the oil in a cast iron casserole dish on a medium heat. Add all the vegetables and cook with the lid on for 10 minutes, stirring occasionally. Add the rosemary and stock. Transfer the casserole to the oven (180°C) and cook for 30 minutes. Remove the lid and cook for a further 15 minutes or until all the vegetables are tender.

SWEETCORN

Purists will have a pan of salted boiling water ready in which to put the freshly picked sweetcorn allowing no time for its sugar content to turn to starch. Served with butter and plenty of salt and pepper, the first sweetcorn to be picked is one of the most memorable treats of the allotment holder's year. Further, sweetcorn makes a good barbecue vegetable. Husks can be tied back to overhang the grill grate and the cobs brushed with oil. It will take about 10 minutes to cook the corn on the grill.

It seems that sweetcorn was not known to the European settlers in America until the eighteenth century. Many Latin American dishes combine corn with green beans or peas. In China, sweetcorn is sold on the streets from pots of boiling water while in the countryside the dried plants are stacked against houses for use as fuel. For me sweetcorn with chillies, tomatoes, and coriander is a perfect combination.

On the allotment, a rectangle of sweetcorn plants is easy and satisfying to grow, provided there is sun, good soil, and they are regularly watered.

Sweetcorn Chowder

There can be all sorts of variations on sweetcorn chowder but I like this basic recipe.

1 large onion, peeled, and finely chopped

1 clove of garlic, peeled and crushed

4 rashers of smoked, streaky bacon, rinds removed, and chopped

60g butter

1 tbsp flour

1 tsp tomato purée

1.2 litres hot chicken stock

300g sweet corn cooked and off the husk (frozen would be fine)

1 large potato, peeled and cut into rough 1cm cubes

1 red chilli deseeded and finely chopped

Salt and freshly ground black pepper

2 tbsp parsley, chopped

60ml double cream

Gently cook the onion, garlic, and bacon in the butter for about five minutes until soft. Stir in the flour and the tomato purée and cook on a low heat for a minute or two. Gradually add the hot chicken stock. Bring to the boil and simmer for five minutes. Add the sweetcorn, potato, and chilli. Season with salt and pepper and simmer for another 20 minutes

Stir in the cream and parsley and return the chowder almost to the boil. Serve immediately.

Sweetcorn with Spiced Butter

When the first helpings of pickings of sweetcorn have been enjoyed, variety can be given by adding chillies, ginger and coriander leaves to the buttery topping.

Finely chop a few fresh chillies, both red and green, a little grated ginger and some coriander leaves. Mix these ingredients into 125g of softened butter and form into a roll. Wrap in cling film and place in the fridge.

When the sweetcorn is ready to serve, take the butter roll from the fridge and unwrap it, then cut it into 2cm slices placing one on the top of each cob.

Sweetcorn and Tomato Salad

Leftover sweetcorn, either boiled or barbecued, can be made into a delightful salad. Slice the kernels off the cob with a sharp knife and put into a bowl with two tomatoes that have been deseeded and diced.

Make a dressing with a jalapeño chilli finely chopped, a chopped clove of garlic, a handful of chopped coriander leaves, three tablespoons of olive oil and one of white wine vinegar, salt and freshly ground black pepper. Cooked green beans or slices of red onion could be added to the salad and the dressing sweetened with a few drops of maple syrup.

Sweetcorn Cakes

2 cobs of sweetcorn, cooked
200g plain flour
2 eggs
1 tsp ground cumin
2 tsp baking powder
Salt and freshly ground black pepper
Corn oil for frying

With a sharp knife, slice the kernels off the cob. Blend all the other ingredients, except the oil, to make a loose batter. Add the corn and mix well.

Heat a little oil in a large frying pan and, using a ladle, pour on the batter, the equivalent of 2-3 tablespoons at a time, to make the cakes. Fry for about three minutes on each side until golden brown.

These cakes are especially good to serve as 'burger buns' with semi-dried tomatoes, prosciutto and a rocket salad.

SWISS CHARD

Bright Lights Swiss chard is a colourful addition to the allotment. I always think of it as happy food, rustic and healthy, combining the earthiness of beetroot and the tannin of spinach. There is also something of the sun and Mediterranean lands in its taste. Chard leaves can be used to make a robust quiche together with red onions, garlic, celery, mixed herbs (mint, sage, and parsley) and a variety of cheeses (Ricotta, Feta, and Pecorino). Toasted pine nuts or raisins can also be added.

In a way Swiss chard is two vegetables, stalk and greens. For all but the smallest leaves, it is usually best to prepare the two parts separately. Slugs love chard and I have noticed ladybirds overwintering in the folds of leaves. Look over the leaves and wash them thoroughly.

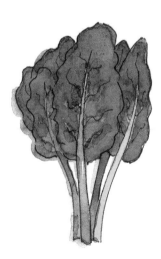

Everyday Swiss Chard

Clean the chard and strip off the green leaves. Tidy up the stalks, cutting them diagonally or into batons. Cook the stalks with a little oil in a large frying pan. Stir to be sure they are coated and then cover the pan and continue cooking gently on a low heat for five to seven minutes. Add the leaves, stir, and cover again. If the chard begins to look too dry, add a tablespoon or two of water but there may be enough moisture left in the leaves. Cook for a further five minutes, or until all parts of the chard are tender. Season. A little lemon juice could also be added before serving.

Swiss Chard Gratin

This is a dish where the stalks come into their own.

500g Swiss chard, stalks only
1 onion, sliced
20g butter
25g plain flour
300ml milk
Salt and freshly ground black pepper
1 tsp thyme leaves
Handful black olives
50g grated Gruyère cheese

Cut the stalks into 4 cm lengths and boil them until just tender.

Melt the butter in a frying pan and gently fry the onion until soft. Add the flour and the thyme leaves. Stir them around for a minute, and then gradually, on a low heat, add the milk to make a white sauce. Season well.

Place the chard stalks in an ovenproof dish, add the black olives. Pour over the onion sauce and spread the Gruyère cheese on top. Bake in a moderate oven for about 20 minutes or until the gratin is browned and bubbling.

TOMATOES

Tomato is such a useful vegetable that this chapter might have been the biggest in the book. In truth, the tomatoes we have grown on the allotment (blight has made growing any tomatoes a challenge) have been so delicious that eating them in a salad or simply seasoned and eaten with cheese is such a delight that they have stood on their own merits, needing few adornments. In Britain, serious tomato growers need a greenhouse.

The smell of home-grown tomatoes freshly picked is irresistible and all the recipes below are chosen with that pleasure in mind. When tomatoes are needed in bulk, I find it best to buy whole boxes from the market.

The name 'tomato' comes from the Nahuatl '*tomatl*' and tomatoes were certainly in Italy by 1544. Tomatoes are related to deadly nightshade and Europeans took some convincing that the bright fruits were safe to eat. It is the leaves that are poisonous. Gerard thought them to be 'of ranke and stinking savour'. Pommodoro – apple of love – it did not take long for aphrodisiacal qualities to be associated with the fruit.

Gazpacho

1kg ripe plum tomatoes, roughly
  chopped
1 green pepper, deseeded and
  roughly chopped
1 onion, roughly chopped
2 cloves garlic, crushed
½ cucumber, peeled (optional)

4–5 cumin seeds
100ml sherry vinegar
150ml olive oil
Chicken stock
Salt and freshly ground
  black pepper

Place the prepared tomatoes, pepper, onion, (and cucumber, if used) and garlic in bowl. Stir in the cumin, vinegar and olive oil. Season well. Leave for several hours for the flavours to mingle. Purée the mixture in a blender and then pass it through a sieve. Mix in cold chicken stock (about 100 ml) to give the right consistency and serve very cold, topped with a garnish of chives or, more extravagantly, dressed crab.

Tomato Salad

Slice whole tomatoes finely and put in a bowl. Make a sauce with olive oil, salt, freshly ground black pepper, and torn basil leaves. If the tomatoes are very ripe a few drops of lemon juice could be added but no vinegar should be used.

Tomatoes à la Provençale

Cut the tops off six large tomatoes, place in a baking dish and pour a little olive oil over each. Lightly add crushed garlic and thyme leaves on the tomatoes, then salt and freshly ground black pepper before adding breadcrumbs. Cook in a roasting oven for about 45 minutes. A light lunch-time dish.

Tomato Sauce for Spaghetti

This sauce epitomizes Italian cooking. It is so simple but all the ingredients must be of the best quality, used generously and cooked with feeling.

Take about 20 ripe tomatoes. Cut off the tops where the stems had been and place the tomatoes flat side down in a large frying pan with a lid. Cook the tomatoes gently with a tablespoon of olive oil until they squash down and the skins can be lifted off. Using a fork, squash them down further, taking away any centres that will not break down. Add two crushed cloves of garlic, salt and pepper to taste and continue to cook the tomatoes – taking the lid on and off as you judge cooking time against thickness of the sauce. In the last minutes of cooking, add finely torn basil leaves.

Cook the spaghetti in a large saucepan with lots of salted water. When ready, lightly drain the spaghetti and mix with the sauce before serving with a bowl of grated Parmesan on the table.

A variation on this sauce is to use oregano in place of basil and add a few tablespoons of Marscapone to the sauce.

Sundried Tomatoes in the Oven

An Aga is best for this recipe. Take lots of ripe tomatoes, cut them in half and score a firm cross over the centres, then pull them further open by pushing from below without breaking the skins. Salt generously and add some ground chilli and dried oregano. Arrange the tomatoes face down on the rack of a large roasting dish and place them in the oven on a very low heat (about 80-100°C) for them to dry. Leave the door of the oven just open. It can take up to 24 hours for the tomatoes to dry but do not rush the process as the tomatoes should dry, as if out in the sun, and not be cooked.

Store them in kilner jars where they will keep for several months. Alternatively, put them in a plastic container in the deep freeze and take them out as required.

GREEN TOMATO CHUTNEY

A recipe that is the saviour of tomatoes that will never ripen before the end of summer and which, to its credit, does taste remarkably good. There is leeway for using shallots or onions, sultanas or raisins, brown or very brown sugar. I have made this chutney every year with whatever is to hand and it has always tasted delicious.

2kg green tomatoes, chopped
750g shallots or onions, peeled and chopped
1 red pepper, deseeded and very finely chopped
500g cooking apples, cored, and finely sliced
250g raisins or sultanas
900ml cider vinegar
4-6 red chillies, deseeded and very finely chopped
500g golden caster sugar or soft brown sugar
2 tsp salt

Put all the ingredients into a preserving pan and bring to the boil, stirring frequently so that nothing sticks to the bottom. Reduce the heat and let the mixture simmer for about 40 minutes, continuing to stir occasionally, until it has thickened but is not too dry. Store in prepared jars for at least a month before using.

Tomato Keftedes

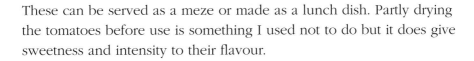

These can be served as a meze or made as a lunch dish. Partly drying the tomatoes before use is something I used not to do but it does give sweetness and intensity to their flavour.

400g small tomatoes
3 tsp tomato paste
4 salad onions, white part only, finely chopped
2 cloves garlic, pressed
1tbsp parsley, finely chopped
3 tbsp mint leaves, finely chopped
1 tsp chilli flakes
300g self-raising flour
Salt and freshly ground black pepper
Olive oil for frying

It is best to prepare the tomatoes the day before. Wash and dry them, cut them in half and lay on the rack of a roasting tray. Sprinkle over plenty of salt. Put them in the oven on a low heat (80-100°C), preferably overnight.

The next day, when the tomatoes are cool, put them into a large bowl and scrunch them up with your fingers so that the skins break and juice runs. Stir in the tomato paste, salad onions, garlic, parsley, mint, chilli flakes and season with salt and pepper. Gradually stir in the flour to form a thick batter.

Heat some oil in a wok or deep sided frying pan. Drop in the tomato paste in spoonfuls. Do not overcrowd but fry the keftedes in batches, turning them until they are brown all over. You will need to watch the heat of the oil as it should not be too hot, burning the outside of the keftedes before the centres are cooked. When ready, drain them on kitchen paper and keep warm until serving.

TOMATO ROULADE WITH RICOTTA AND BASIL

This is an impressive dish for a summer lunch party which needs tasty, ripe, tomatoes to give sufficient flavour. It takes time to make but preparation can be done in stages over several hours and once mastered, it is very simple and satisfying to make.

2 shallots, peeled and chopped

2 cloves garlic, peeled and chopped

2 tbsp olive oil

500g tomatoes, skinned and chopped

1 tbsp tomato purée

Fresh thyme

1 tsp sugar

4 eggs separated

Salt and freshly ground black pepper

2 tbsp black mustard seeds

Stuffing:

150g Ricotta

Handful basil, finely chopped

Using a frying pan with a lid, gently fry the shallots and garlic in the oil until soft. Add the tomatoes, purée, sugar and leaves taken from a few sprigs of thyme. Season generously and, using the lid, let the mixture simmer, stirring occasionally, until it is very thick. This will take time but do not rush or the mixture will burn. Allow to cool, then blend in a food processor. This step can be done well in advance.

Line a Swiss-roll tin or large roasting tray with baking parchment.

Separate the eggs and blend the egg yolks in a food processor with the tomato mixture until smooth. Whisk the egg whites until stiff and carefully fold them into the tomato mixture. Spread onto the tin and bake in an oven at 180°C for 15-20 minutes, until firm. Leave to cool but place a damp cloth on a roasting rack over the roulade to keep it moist.

Turn the roulade onto a sheet of greaseproof paper on which the mustard seeds have been spread. Mix the Ricotta with the basil and spread over the middle of the roulade. With a sharp knife score firmly a few centimeters in from one long edge. Starting with this edge, and using the greaseproof paper to help, roll the roulade up tightly.

Sprinkle over a little more chopped basil or some grated Parmesan if you choose. Place on a serving dish and cut slices.

TURNIPS

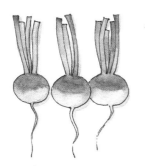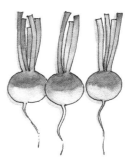

Turnips are among the first cultivated vegetables. Pliny the Elder declared that the 'utility (of the turnip) surpasses that of any other plant'. The Romans are known to have been growing turnips in France by AD42 and it is likely that they brought them to Britain. They would have been used for animal fodder as well as culinary use.

Charles Townshend, 2nd Viscount Townshend of Raynham (1645-1738) more popularly known as Turnip Townshend, revolutionized British farming by introducing the rotation system.

As highly rated as they once were, turnips are not much in fashion today. Bought turnips tend to be big and strongly flavoured. By growing your own and picking them small, the purple tinged turnips become more like a radish, to which they are related. The most tender can be thinly sliced and added to salads. The classic dish requiring turnips is Navarin of Lamb.

There is no section in this book for kohl rabi. In most recipes they can be substituted for turnips. I like to use them sliced, alternating with potato in a gratin or raw, grated with carrots and celeriac, in a slaw. Best of all, I like to serve them freshly picked from the allotment, simply boiled and buttered.

GLAZED TURNIPS

This dish is delicious with roast lamb. The leaves should not be omitted as they do give an extra dimension.

500g small turnips with leaves
Salt and freshly ground black pepper
A good knob of butter
1tbsp chopped chervil

Take the leaves from the turnips, wash and put them to one side. Give the turnips a wash but leave on their skins. Put in a saucepan, cover with water, and add the salt and butter. Bring to the boil, then simmer for about 10 minutes until tender.

Add the leaves and the chervil, season with pepper, and simmer with lid off for a further 2-3 minutes.

Drain and serve immediately.

PASTRIES, SAUCES AND DESSERTS

A VERY GOOD PASTRY FOR QUICHES

Which pastry to make for a quiche is very much a personal choice. At the moment this is my favourite. Inspiration came from Elizabeth David's recipe for Tarte à L'Onion in *French Provincial Cooking*.

250g plain flour
125g butter, chilled
1 egg yolk
Chilled water
Pinch of salt

Put the flour in a large bowl and add the butter cut into smallish chunks and a pinch of salt. Working with light fingers, mix the butter into the flour. Add the egg yolk and a tablespoon or two of the chilled water, enough to form a dough. The flour will leave the sides of the bowl. Press gently into a ball. It doesn't have to be perfect as lumps of butter should still be obvious.

Place the dough on a lightly floured board and, with the heel of your hand, form it into a very rough pastry. Gather it up and repeat the process. Gather it up again and form the dough into a ball. Wrap in cling film and store in the fridge for at least an hour before use.

PUFF PASTRY

I learnt how to make puff pastry on a course by Ghalid Assyb held at Richard Bertinet's Cookery School in Bath.

250g plain flour
125ml very cold water
25g melted butter
1 tsp lemon juice
200g chilled butter
Pinch of salt

Sift the flour into a large bowl and make a well in the centre. Add the water, salt, lemon juice and melted butter. Using your fingertips, bring in the flour little by little until you have a rough ball. Turn out onto a work surface and knead the dough for several minutes until it is smooth. Form into a ball, cut a deep cross on the top, wrap in cling film and put into the fridge for at least an hour.

To make the chilled butter soft while still in a pat, place it between two pieces of greaseproof paper on a large board and beat it with a rolling pin until the butter is about 1 cm thick and formed into a square. Keep cool until ready for use.

On a lightly floured surface, roll out the dough, turning it as you work, to make a quatrefoil shape – a rectangle, the size of the flattened butter, with looping sides so that it looks a little like an opened out envelope. Place the butter on top of the rectangle, and fold over the four loops to cover it.

Roll the pastry into a rectangle. It helps to always think of this pastry as a book, with the longest sides to left and right. Then fold the top third down and the bottom third up to make a parcel of three even layers. Turn the pastry at right angles and repeat the rolling and folding twice more, always trying to keep the corners square. Wrap the pastry in cling film and chill for 30 minutes.

Repeat the rolling, folding in three, turning, process twice more, and then put the dough into the fridge for at least an hour.

Puff pastry can be used to make savory dishes. My favourite is a light lunch dish made from two slices of puff pastry between which is sandwiched cooked and drained finely chopped spinach with Ricotta and a hint of nutmeg, served hot with a tomato sauce poured over.

MILLE FEUILLES

By my reckoning, the puff pastry in my recipe above has 486 layers.

On a lightly floured board, roll out the puff pastry, as given in the above recipe, until it is 5mm thick. Prick it over with a fork. Place it on a baking tray lined with baking parchment and put the tray in a cold spot for at least 15 minutes.

Before baking the pastry, in order to stop it from rising, cover the top with a second baking tray. Bake for about 20 minutes in a hot oven (200°C), then reduce the temperature to 170°C, remove the top baking tray and continue to cook for a further five minutes or until the pastry is golden brown. Transfer to a wire rack to cool.

Many fine deserts can be created by cutting the pastry into three equal pieces and building up with layers of raspberries, poached figs or poached, stoned apricots alternating with generous layers of whipped cream or crème Anglaise (see page 217). Top with more fruit and icing sugar.

Mayonnaise

There is no mystique about making mayonnaise although it is not something to be done in a rush or while under pressure. I use a handheld electric whisk on a medium setting but some cooks insist that nothing but a hand whisk or just a spoon, will do.

2 egg yolks
About 300ml olive oil
Salt and freshly ground black pepper
Pinch English mustard
Juice of 1 lemon

Put the egg yolks into a bowl and add a little seasoning and the mustard. Give the egg yolks a light whisk to break them up and then, very carefully, begin to introduce the olive oil. Start with no more than a few drops and whisk them in carefully before adding more. After a while the sauce begins to thicken and you can start to be more liberal with the amount of oil added. It is at this point that Elizabeth David's words of caution come to mind: *"Not at a gallop"*. Continue adding the oil until the infusion becomes very thick. Lemon juice can now be added until the mayonnaise has reached the desired consistency. Check the seasoning. Transfer to a clean bowl, cover with cling film and store in the fridge.

Mayonnaise should be made with the freshest eggs. If it is to be kept for a day or two, stir in two tablespoons of boiled water at the end of making it. This prevents both separation and an oily surface forming.

Classic uses of mayonnaise are:
Aïoli where crushed garlic is added to the mayonnaise.
Sauce Marie Rose Tomato ketchup and Tabasco are added to the mayonnaise and a few drops of Cognac or aquavit are optional. Serve with prawns in a salad.
Mayonnaise with puréed watercress has a place in many summer salads. I like it on top of hard boiled eggs or with slices of cold veal.
Devilled eggs are hard boiled eggs cut in half and topped with mayonnaise to which a little Dijon mustard and lemon juice have been added.

BÉCHAMEL SAUCE

❧

Described by Escoffier as one of the 'five mother sauces', Elizabeth David calls it 'rather dull' but it is the basis of many more interesting sauces and dishes such as Mornay sauce and Veal Orlov. Richard Olney in *Simple French Food* wonders 'that those who share the fashionable distaste for flour-bound sauces suffer no pangs of regret for having banned the friendly béchamel from their tables'.

75g butter
60g plain flour
1 litre milk

Heat the butter in a small saucepan. As it starts to foam, take the pan off the heat and stir in the flour. Add a little milk and return the pan to a gentle heat. Little by little stir in the rest of the milk (or enough to give the consistency required) and continue to cook for five minutes or more. Richard Olney says 'a minimum of an hour is best'. But the point is made that the sauce needs to cook beyond thickening to lose its floury taste.

Salt, white pepper and a hint of nutmeg or a bay leaf are the traditional flavourings.

SABLÉE PASTRY

This is a melt in the mouth pastry for sweet tarts but is crumbly and can be frustrating to make.

250g plain flour
200g butter, chilled
100g icing sugar
2 egg yolks

Heap the flour onto a work surface and make a well in the middle. Cut the butter into small chunks and put them in the well with the icing sugar. Working lightly, rub the butter into the flour and icing sugar and then add the egg yolks. Mix until you have formed a ball of dough. (if using large egg yolks you may need to add a very little extra flour.)

Return the dough to the work surface and, using the heel of your hand, work the dough, pushing it away from you three or four times until it is smooth. Reform into a ball and wrap in cling film. Store in the fridge for at least an hour before use.

RICH SHORT CRUST PASTRY

250g plain flour
175g very cold butter
1 egg yolk
Approx. 1 tbsp cold water
A pinch of salt

Sift the flour and salt into a bowl and add the butter cut into chunks. With your finger tips rub the butter into the flour. Add the egg yolk and enough water to make a dough. Knead lightly for a few minutes. Form into a ball and wrap in cling film to chill before use.

Sweet crust pastry

Use the recipe above adding a tablespoon of caster sugar with the egg yolk.

Rice Pudding

✤

I defend rice pudding and all milk puddings. In the first class restaurant of the *Titanic* tapioca pudding was served to diners on the fateful evening that she went down.

I give recipes for hot and cold rice pudding. Both versions can be served with stewed fruit, jam or fresh fruit, puréed or finely sliced.

Hot rice pudding:

500ml full fat milk
3 tbsp pudding rice
2 tbsp caster sugar

Stir all the ingredients around in a well-buttered oven proof dish. Grate nutmeg on top and dot with shavings of butter. Cook at a low temperature (120°C) for two to three hours. Stir once or twice during the first hour of cooking

Cold rice pudding:

100ml double cream
800ml full fat milk
½ vanilla pod
Pinch of salt
100g pudding rice
50g caster sugar
2 egg yolks

Slowly heat the milk, cream, vanilla and a pinch of salt in a pan until almost boiling then add the rice and cook very slowly, stirring often, for 15 minutes.

Whisk the egg yolks with the sugar and whisk into the rice mixture. Ideally continue to cook in a bain marie but use a double saucepan until the rice is cooked (about 20 minutes). Chill before use.

MERINGUES

The making of meringues is very personal. Any variety of tips and added ingredients work for some but not others.

Tips include, warming the sugar, adding a teaspoon of corn flour or a few drops of white wine vinegar in the final stages of making the meringues. All I can suggest is that you try until you find the method that suits you. There is even disagreement in the type of sugar; some use all caster sugar and others a mixture of caster and granulated sugar but in all of this, the one constant is the measure of ingredients. For every egg white use two tablespoons (i.e. two ounces) of sugar.

I start by whisking the egg whites until stiff, then adding warmed sugar slowly, whisking between each addition. Even such guidance may not suit you; in Italy the sugar and egg whites are whisked together from the beginning.

However the process is reached, the meringue mixture needs to become thick and glossy. Using two desert spoons, place each meringue, well-spaced, onto a baking tray lined with baking parchment. Bake in an oven heated to 120°C for about two hours until the meringues are crisp but not coloured.

Meringues can keep for a week or two in an airtight tin. They are an easy pudding, served with double cream and with strawberries, wood strawberries or raspberries scattered on top.

PANNACOTTA

550ml single cream
750ml full fat milk
1 vanilla pod, slit
100g caster sugar
5 gelatine leaves

Soak the gelatine leaves in cold water until soft. Pour the cream and milk into a large pan and add the sugar and vanilla pod. Heat gently but do not let it boil.

Squeeze the softened gelatine leaves and add them to the milk mixture. Stir until the gelatine is completely dissolved. Remove the vanilla pod.

Pour the mixture into a lightly oiled mould or ramekin dishes and chill for at least two hours. To serve, briefly put the mould or ramekins into shallow very hot water and then invert onto a plate. Alternatively, pannacotta can be served in cups. Either way, decorate with fresh or lightly stewed fruit.

Crème Anglaise

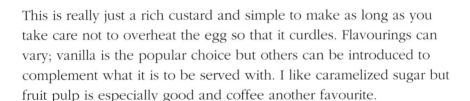

This is really just a rich custard and simple to make as long as you take care not to overheat the egg so that it curdles. Flavourings can vary; vanilla is the popular choice but others can be introduced to complement what it is to be served with. I like caramelized sugar but fruit pulp is especially good and coffee another favourite.

150ml full fat milk
150ml double cream
1 egg and one egg yolk
2 tbsp sugar

Bring the milk and cream to boiling point with the flavouring (if vanilla, seeds taken from a pod would be better than essence) and put to one side on a very low heat for 20 minutes or so.

Beat the eggs with the sugar. Strain on a little of the milk and cream and beat well. By degrees add all the liquid, beating well between additions. Pour into a clean milk pan and stir over a low heat until the sauce is thick enough to coat the back of a wooden spoon.

Put in a basin, cover with clingfilm and keep cool before using. Either serve immediately as a rich custard or pour the crème into a basin, cover with cling film and chill before using.

CHEESECAKE

I love this cheesecake which I learnt to cook at Signe Johansen's course at Richard Bertinet's Cookery School. I have since cooked it often and served it with strawberries and raspberries (both fresh and stewed), cooked plums, cherries, and rhubarb. It never fails.

Base:

200g ginger biscuits or similar
50g melted butter
50g demerara sugar
Pinch of ground cinnamon

Cheesecake:

4 eggs, separated
175g caster sugar
240ml soured cream
1 tsp vanilla essence
2 tbsp corn flour
Pinch of salt
240g full-fat cream cheese

Lightly oil a 23cm loose bottomed cake tin and set aside.

To make the base, crumble the biscuits and put them in a large bowl. Mix in the other ingredients for the base. Tip the base mixture into the cake tin. Press down firmly and evenly. Store in the cool.

Beat the egg yolks in a large bowl with 125g of the sugar until light and frothy. Add the sour cream, vanilla, cornflour and salt. By degrees, beat in the cream cheese, a large spoonful at a time.

Whisk the egg whites with the remaining sugar until stiff peaks are formed. Add one large spoonful of this to the cheese cake mixture to loosen it and then gently fold in the rest.

Spoon the mixture onto the base and spread even with a pallet knife. Bake in a cool oven (around 160°C) for 45-50 minutes or until the surface feels firm. The cheesecake should only turn the palest brown, so check it carefully and turn down the heat if it is taking on too much colour.

Let the cake cool slowly. I even let it rest in the warming oven of the Aga for five minutes or so to before bringing it out of the oven. The cake may split but, with luck, any fault line might be used as a main cutting line or could be buried under fruit for serving.

WAFFLES

I find making waffles a good way to entertain and engage small children. This is a very good recipe, taken from Signe Johansen's excellent book, *Scandilicious*.

230g plain flour
¼ tsp baking powder
70g caster sugar
Pinch of salt
70g melted butter

70ml water
150g soured cream
100ml whole milk
2 eggs, beaten
1–2 tsp vanilla essence

Sift the dry ingredients into a large bowl, and then stir in the rest. Stir it together until it becomes a sticky batter, reluctant to drop from a spoon. Set the batter aside for at least half an hour for the flour to swell.

Butter the waffle iron and let it heat up until the butter bubbles and then pour a ladle of the waffle mixture over the sections of the iron. Close the lid and let cook until the waffles are brown and crispy on the outside. Sprinkle over sugar and serve hot.

Vanilla Ice Cream

300ml single cream
300ml double cream
4 egg yolks
1 vanilla pod
Caster sugar

Slowly bring the single cream, with the vanilla pod added, to the boil. Cover and leave to infuse over a very low heat for about 20 minutes.

Beat the egg yolks and whisk in a little of the warm cream. Add to the remaining cream in the pan and, over a low heat, stir until it is custard-like.

Sweeten to taste, remove the vanilla pod and strain this custard mixture into the double cream. Pour into the ice cream maker and leave until set. Remove from the freezer at least half an hour before use.

Pancakes

I like pancakes stuffed with puréed apple and thick purées of plums with fromage frais.

300ml full fat milk
125g plain flour
2 eggs
A generous knob of melted butter

Whisk all the ingredients together – they should be the consistency of single cream – and allow to stand for at least half an hour.

Use the first pancake as a 'taster'. Lightly butter a non-stick frying pan and put on a medium heat. Pour in a thin layer of batter. Move the pan around so that the batter covers the surface. Once the batter has set, flip or turn the pancake to cook on the other side. There should be no more than a hint of the batter turning brown in cooking.

Dust with sugar, add a filling if required and roll up.

CHOCOLATE ROULADE

This recipe comes from Mary Berry's *New Aga Cookbook.* It is a great success at large lunch parties and, despite the large quantities, is very easy to make.

275g plain good quality chocolate
275g caster sugar
10 eggs, separated

To finish:
450ml double cream
Icing sugar

Grease and line a roasting tin with baking parchment. Break the chocolate into pieces and place in a double saucepan to melt slowly and then allow to cool a little. In a large bowl, whisk the egg whites with the sugar until stiff but not dry and carefully fold in the chocolate. Turn onto the prepared roasting tin and carefully smooth over the surface.

Bake at 175–180°C for about 25 minutes until firm to the touch. Turn the roulade during cooking to be sure that it bakes evenly.

Take the roulade from the oven and place over it a cooling rack (or grill from a roasting pan) with a damp clean cloth spread over the top. Leave until the roulade is cool.

Whip the cream. Dust a large sheet of greaseproof paper with icing sugar, turn the roulade onto it. Peel off the parchment paper. Score a line a few centimeters in along one long side of the roulade, spread over the cream and, starting with the long scored side, roll up the roulade using the greaseproof paper to help.

Dust with more icing sugar and serve.

ACKNOWLEDGMENTS

Without the 'team' of Carrie Hill, Sally Geeve, and Rosemary Cole, with their drawing, design, editing and indexing skills, this book would never have come about. I am very grateful and thank them for putting me right in so many ways. My husband, William, has, I think, enjoyed the task of tasting recipes and been very supportive. For the greater part, he has been long suffering and I must thank him for being the potato peeler of the household as well as a much wiser gardener than me. I am greatly indebted to Rosie Sansome and Rodney Lyons for their special skills and to Mike Pugh for seeing the book through publication. Simon Strawbridge gave technical help which was much appreciated.

Recipes do not invent themselves and I must first thank friends who have given inspiration. In Bath, Penny Dalrymple-Smith has given me lots of ideas and recipes as well as aprons to match the occasion. From the French group Marie-Noëlle Davis, David Cheadle, Connie Cornforth, and Bärbl Gascoigne have all kindly given the recipes for the dishes they bring to the parties and Di Cray has given allotment advice as well as recipes and produce from her superb plot. I am grateful to Margaret Kelland for introducing me to runner bean chutney. I have fond memories of her parents' vegetable garden. David Kelland gave useful advice about drying apples and tomatoes. My cousin, Ann Butler, has helped with the history of food as has Louise Pavey who also gave recipes and let me pick white currants. Carin Nelander advised on Scandinavian food.

Eades, our greengrocer, is legendary. The family firm now has its fifth generation and supplies the local restaurants as well as its regular customers. Bartletts, the butchers, serve me well. Thanks are due to Julie Payne of Pennybatch, near Wells, my 'Egg Lady', and the stables nearby at Burcott. Gordon Wallford deserves special thanks for having helped on my allotment for many years. Many more deserve thanks; David Pratt, Peter Robinson of NAWB, Marshalls, and Suttons Seeds who took trouble to answer my queries.

Food writers I especially admire are Anna del Conte, Jane Grigson, Donna Hay, Mark Hix, Simon Hopkinson, Yotam Ottolenghi, Sarah Raven, Claudia Roden, and Nigel Slater. Elizabeth David's recipes still ring in my ears; I never fail to whisper 'not at a gallop' as I add oil while making mayonnaise. Jocasta Innes's *Pauper's Cookbook* was a revelation for having the right mix of survival instinct and fun. Richard Bertinet's cookery school in Bath has given inspiration. I especially enjoyed the days spent on courses with Monisha Bharadwaj and Signe Johansen. Anna Pavord's garden column in *The Independent* keeps me up to date with allotment and garden tasks.

Overheard recipes, snippets of advice, anonymous now yellowed newspaper cuttings from years ago, this book is a distillation of my favourite recipes.

BIBLIOGRAPHY

Berry, Mary, *Mary Berry's Baking Bible* (BBC Books 2009)

Editor-in-chief Caroline Bretherton, *The Allotment Cookbook through the year* (Dorling Kindersley 2011)

Carluccio, Antonio, *An Invitation to Italian Cooking* (Pavilion Boks Limited, 1986)

Carrier, Robert, *The Robert Carrier Cookbook* (Sphere Books1967)

Coumont, Alain and Gabriel, Jean-Pierre, *Le Pain Quotidien Cookbook* (Mitchell Beazley, 2013)

David, Elizabeth, *French Provincial Cooking* (Penguin Books 1969)

David, Elizabeth, *Italian Food* (Penguin Books 1977)

David, Elizabeth, *Spices, Salt and Aromatics in the English Kitchen* (Penguin Books 1970)

David, Elizabeth, *Summer Cooking* (Penguin Books 1965)

Del Conte, Anna, *Classic Food of Northern Italy* (Pavilion Books Limited 2004)

Del Conte, Anna, *Italian Kitchen* (Square Peg 2012)

Del Conte, Anna, *The Best of Anna del Conte* (Vintage 2006)

Demuth, Rachel, *Green Seasons Cookbook* (Chupi Publishing 2006)

Dickson Wright, Clarissa and Scott, Johnny, *Sunday Roast* (Headline Book Publishing 2002)

Fearnley-Whittingstall, Hugh, *The River Cottage Meat Book* (Hodder & Stoughton 2004)

Fearnley-Whittingstall, Hugh, *River Cottage Light and Easy* (Bloomsbury Publishing Plc 2014)

Grigson, Jane, *Jane Grigson's Fruit Book* (Michael Joseph 1982)

Hart, Carolyn, *Cooks' Books* (Simon & Schuster 2006)

Hay, Donna, *New Fast Food* (HarperCollins 2005)

Hix, Mark, *British Seasonal Food* (Quadrille Publishing Ltd 2008)

Hix, Mark, *Mark Hix The Collection* (Quadrille Publishing Ltd 2013)

Hopkinson, Simon, *Week In Week Out* (Quadrille Publishing Ltd 2007)

Huang, Ching-He, *Chinese Food in Minutes* (HarperCollins 2009)

Hume, Rosemary and Downes, Muriel, *Cordon Bleu Desserts and Puddings* (Penguin Books 1976)

Innes, Jocasta, *The Pauper's Cookbook* (Penguin Books 1971)

Johansen, Signe, *Scandilicious* (Saltyard Books 2011)

Johansen, Signe, *Scandilicious Baking* (Saltyard Books 2012)

Lawson, Nigella, *How to Eat* (Chatto & Windus 1999)

Mabey, Richard, *Flora Britannica* (Sinclair Stevenson 1996)

Mabey, Richard, *Food for Free* (Harper Collins Publishers 1989)

Olney, Richard, *Simple French Food* (Grub Street, 2003)

Ottolenghi, Yotam, *Jerusalem* (Ebury Press 2012)

Ottolenghi, Yotam, *Plenty* (Ebury Press 2010)

Roden, Claudia, *Arabesque* (Michael Joseph 2005)

Roden, Claudia, *The Food of Italy* (Square Peg 2014)

Roden, Claudia, *Tamarind & Saffron* (Penguin Books 1999)

Wild at Heart, *Hedgerow Cookbook* (Pavilion 2013)

INDEX

A

aïoli 97

almonds
 plum and almond tart 158
 raspberry and almond Eve's
  pudding 172
 redcurrant Mazarin tart 89
 rhubarb and orange
  cake 182

anchovies
 anchovy and egg dressing
  133
 broccoli with pasta 50
 Jansson's temptation 166
 pissaladière 136

apples 11-18
 apple and blackberry pie 14
 apple jelly 18
 apple snow 12
 baked apples 12
 blackberry and apple jelly
  110
 crumble 181
 damson chutney 107
 dried apples 15
 green tomato chutney 204
 hot apple and Calvados
  soufflé 13
 mincemeat for Christmas 15
 pear and apple chutney 150
 tarte aux pommes 17
 tarte tatin 16

apricots, pie filling 14

artichokes, globe 19-22
 artichokes alla Italiana 21
 artichokes Barigoule 22
 artichokes, parboiled and
  braised 20
 artichokes, peas and broad
  beans 21
 Provençal artichokes 22
 raw artichoke salad 20

artichokes, Jerusalem 23-24
 artichoke and potato soup
  24
 sautéed artichokes 24

asparagus 25-32
 asparagus and goat's cheese
  tarts 32
 asparagus in a salad of pea
  shoots 26
 asparagus soup 28

asparagus with chopped
 hard boiled eggs
 (asparagus mimosa) 31
asparagus with cream and
 pasta 27
chargrilled asparagus 26
Chinese asparagus 29
lemon butter sauce for 27
oriental sauce for 29
pickled asparagus 30

avocados
 Penny's carrot and
 spinach terrine 58

B

bacon
 dandelion salad 118
 Italian cabbage 55
 red cabbage with pears 56
 sweetcorn chowder 197

basil
 rocket or basil pesto sauce
  114
 tomato roulade with Ricotta
  and basil 206

beans, runner, French, Blue
 Lake and others 37-40
 see also broad beans
 bean salad 38
 borlotti bean bruschetta 39
 borlotti ratatouille 39
 Chinese beans 38
 mixed beans with spices 35
 ribollita 67
 runner bean chutney 40
 wilted spinach with
  cannellini beans and
  tomatoes 188

béchamel sauce 213

beef, borscht 42

beetroot 41-46
 beetroot and chocolate cake
  46
 beetroot Bourguignon 44
 beetroot relish 45
 beetroot with allspice 42
 borscht 42
 crisps 143
 everyday roasted pumpkin
  or squash 168
 Greek beetroot salad 43
 pickled beetroot 45

thyme-roasted beetroot 44
warm winter vegetable salad
 141

blackberries
 apple and blackberry pie 14
 apple jelly 18
 autumn fruit coulis 108
 blackberry and apple jelly
  110
 mousse 175
 pavlova 174
 summer pudding 106

blackcurrants see currants,
 black, red and white

borage 113

borlotti beans 39

brambles see blackberries

brandy snaps 102

bread
 chicory gratin 76
 cucumber sandwiches 84
 French onion soup 135
 Jansson's temptation 166
 parsnips Molly Parkin 144
 ribollita 67

broad beans 33-36
 artichokes, peas and broad
  beans 21
 broad bean purée 36
 broad beans and Pecorino
  antipasti 34
 falafel 34
 mixed beans with spices 35
 peas and beans with new
  potatoes 162
 soupe Menerboise 78
 young broad beans cooked
  with onion 36

broccoli 47-50
 broccoli and Stilton soup 48
 broccoli smoothies 47
 broccoli with pasta 50
 purple spouting broccoli
  with pickled walnuts and
  Pecorino cheese 49
 salad of calabrese stalks 49

Brussels sprouts 51-52
 Brussels sprouts with
  chestnuts 52
 Brussels sprouts with
  mustard 52

bulgar wheat
    parsnip, carrot and bulgar
      wheat salad 141
    tabbouleh 119

C
cabbage 53-56
    Chinese stir fried cabbage
      55
    everyday cabbage 54
    Italian cabbage 55
    mango coleslaw 54
    red cabbage with pears 56
cakes
    beetroot and chocolate cake
      46
    carrot cake with lime
      Mascarpone icing 60
    Springfield cake (pear and
      ginger sponge) 147–148
calabrese *see* broccoli
cannellini beans with wilted
  spinach and tomatoes **188**
capers, cauliflower,
  radicchio and caper salad
  74
carrots 57-60
    beetroot Bourguignon 44
    carrot and cumin salad 59
    carrot cake with lime
      Mascarpone icing 60
    carrot salad with chilli 59
    casserole of winter
      vegetables 195
    everyday carrots 58
    everyday roasted pumpkin
      or squash 168
    everyday swedes 195
    mango coleslaw 54
    mashed parsnips and carrots
      143
    parsnip, carrot and bulgar
      wheat salad 141
    Penny's carrot and spinach
      terrine 58
    piccalilli 64
    ribollita 67
    roast chicory tart 75
    warm winter vegetable salad
      141
casserole
    of winter vegetables 195
cauliflower 61-64
    cauliflower, radicchio and
      caper salad 74
    everyday Indian cauliflower
      and potatoes 63

    piccalilli 64
    roasted cauliflower and
      hazelnut salad 62
caviar 164
cavolo nero and kale 65-68
    cavolo nero sauce for penne
      68
    colcannon 66
    ribollita 67
celery and celeriac 69-72
    braised celery hearts 70
    celeriac and thyme gratin 71
    chilled lettuce and celery
      soup 130
    classic rémoulade 72
    cream of celery soup 70
    Indian celeriac rémoulade 72
    nettle soup 121
    ribollita 67
Cheddar cheese
    homity pie 165
cheese
    asparagus and goat's cheese
      tarts 32
    asparagus in a salad of pea
      shoots 26
    blue cheese salad dressing
      132
    broccoli and Stilton soup 48
    cannelloni with peas and
      Gorgonzola 155
    chicory gratin 76
    courgette and goat's cheese
      soufflé 80
    French onion soup 135
    homity pie 165
    Lancashire cheese and
      onion pie 137
    Parmesan and thyme straws
      122
    parsnips Molly Parkin 144
    pear and blue cheese salad
      146
    pumpkin with Raclette 169
    Swiss chard gratin 199
    Welsh rarebit leeks 127
cheesecake 218
cherries
    redcurrant, white currant
      and cherry fool 91
chestnuts
    Brussels sprouts with 52
chicken
    chicken liver pâté with
      thyme 117
    roast chicken stuffed with
      courgettes under the skin 81

chickpeas
    hummus 98
    parsnip, chickpea and
      saffron soup 142
chicory
    endive, radicchio and
      Treviso 73–76
    cauliflower, radicchio and
      caper salad 74
    chicory gratin 76
    grilled radicchio or Treviso 76
    radicchio and prawn salad 74
    roast chicory tart 75
chillies
    sweetcorn with spiced butter
      197
chives, egg and chive
  sandwiches 114
    leeks vinaigrette 127
    prawns and chives smörgås
      114
chocolate roulade 221
chutneys *see* pickles
colcannon 66
coriander
    herb stuffing for fish 120
    sweetcorn with spiced butter
      197
    tabbouleh 119
courgettes and marrow 77-82
    courgette and Feta fritters 82
    courgette and goat's cheese
      soufflé 80
    courgette flower tempura 78
    courgette soup 78
    marrow salad 79
    roast chicken stuffed with
      courgettes under the skin 81
cranachan 178
crème Anglaise 217
cucumbers 83-86
    cucumber salad 85
    cucumber sandwiches 84
    experimenting with
      cucumber 85
    gazpacho 202
    piccalilli 64
    pickled cucumbers with
      garlic and mustard seeds 86
    radicchio and prawn salad 74
    salad of fennel, cucumber
      and radish 94
    tabbouleh 119
    tarator 84
**currants, black, red and white
87-92**
    blackcurrant coulis 88

blackcurrant jam 88
pavlova 174
pie filling 14
redcurrant jelly 92
redcurrant Mazarin tart 89
redcurrant, white currant
    and cherry fool 91
summer pudding 106
vanilla bean brulée with
    blackcurrants 90

D
damsons
    apple jelly 18
    autumn fruit coulis 108
    damson chutney 107
    damson sorbet 109
    mousse 175
dandelion salad 118
Drambuie 178
drinks
    broccoli smoothies 47
    elderflower cordial 104
    mint tea 118
    rhubarb cordial 184
    sloe gin 110
    walnut leaf liqueur 111

E
eggs
    anchovy and egg dressing
        133
    asparagus with chopped
    hard boiled eggs (asparagus
        mimosa) 31
    borscht 42
    devilled aggs 212
    egg and chive sandwiches
        114
    leeks vinaigrette 127
    pommes Lyonnaise plus
        163
elderberries
    apple jelly 18
    autumn fruit coulis 108
    elderberry dressing for game
        105
    summer pudding 106
elderflowers
    elderflower cordial 104
    elderflower fritters 105
    flavouring for milk puddings
        113
    with gooseberries 99
Emmental cheese, French
    onion soup 135
endive see chicory, endive,
    radicchio and Treviso

F
falafel 34, 36
fava beans see broad beans
fennel 93-96
    cod with fennel, leeks and
        tomatoes 95
    marinated fennel 94
    Mark Hix's galette au fenouil
        96
    radicchio and prawn salad
        74
    roast chicory tart 75
    salad of fennel and orange
        94
    salad of fennel, cucumber
        and radish 94
Feta cheese
    asparagus in a salad of pea
        shoots 26
    courgette and Feta fritters
        82
    parsnip, carrot and bulgar
        wheat salad 141
    roast pumpkin risotto 170
figs, caramel 112
    figs in mille feuilles 211
fish
    cod with fennel, leeks and
        tomatoes 95
    gooseberry sauce for
        mackerel 100
    herb stuffing for fish 120
flummery, raspberry 177
French beans see beans,
    runner, French, Blue Lake
    and others

G
garlic 97-98
    aïoli 97
    hummus 98
    linguini with garlic and chilli
        98
    pickled cucumbers with
        garlic and mustard seeds 86
gazpacho 202
geraniums, scented as
    flavouring for milk puddings
        113
ginger
    pear and apple chutney 150
    pumpkin and ginger soup
        168
    Springfield cake (pear and
        ginger sponge) 147–148
    sweetcorn with spiced butter
        197

goat's cheese
    asparagus and goat's cheese
        tarts 32
    courgette and goat's cheese
        soufflé 80
gooseberries 99-102
    crumble 181
    gooseberry fool 101
    gooseberry ice cream with
        brandy snaps 102
    gooseberry jam 101
    gooseberry sauce for
        mackerel 100
Gorgonzola cheese
    cannelloni with peas and
        Gorgonzola 155
grapefruit, rhubarb and
    grapefruit jam 183
greengages see plums and
    greengages
Gruyère cheese
    French onion soup 135
    parsnips Molly Parkin 144
    pumpkin with Raclette 169
    Swiss chard gratin 200
hazelnuts, roasted cauliflower
    and hazelnut salad 62
hedgerow fruits 103-112
herbs and weeds 113-122
horseradish
    beetroot relish 45
    horseradish sauce 116

I
ice creams
    damson sorbet 109
    gooseberry ice cream with
        brandy snaps 102
    raspberry ripple ice cream 176
    rhubarb ice cream 180
    vanilla ice cream 220

J
jams and jellies
    apple jelly 18
    blackberry and apple jelly 110
    blackcurrant jam 88
    gooseberry jam 101
    medlar jelly 109
    plum jam 157
    redcurrant jelly 92
    rhubarb and grapefruit jam
        183
    unboiled raspberry jam 175

K

kale *see* cavolo nero and kale
kohl rabi 207

L

Lancashire cheese and onion
    pie 137
leeks 123-128
    asparagus soup 28
    chilled lettuce and celery
        soup 130
    cod with fennel, leeks and
        tomatoes 95
    colcannon 66
    everyday leeks 124
    leek fritters with soured
        cream dressing 128
    leek pie (flamiche) 126
    leek tart (tarte aux poireaux)
        125
    leeks vinaigrette 127
    nettle soup 121
    pea and lovage soup 152
    Vichyssoise 124
    Welsh rarebit leeks 127
lemon butter sauce and
    asparagus 27
lentils, Puy 44
lettuces 129-133
    anchovy and egg dressing
        for 133
    chilled lettuce and celery
        soup 130
    lettuce and pea soup 131
    lettuce salad 132
    radicchio and prawn salad 74
    steamed peas and lettuce
        133
limes, carrot cake with lime
    Mascarpone icing 60
lovage
    chilled lettuce and celery
        soup 130
    pea and lovage soup 152

M

mango coleslaw 54
marrows *see* courgettes and
    marrow
Marsala
    raspberries and zabaglione
        172
    Ricotta al forno with
        strawberries and Marsala
        193
Mascarpone cheese
    carrot cake with lime

Mascarpone icing 60
    pea and mint risotto 154
mayonnaise 212
medlar jelly 109
melon and Parma ham with
    strawberry salsa 190
meringues 216
mint
    cold pea and mint soup 152
    mint sauce 118
    mint tea 118
    parsnip, carrot and bulgar
        wheat salad 141
    pea and mint risotto 154
    purée of fresh peas 152
    tabbouleh 119
mushrooms, parsley-stuffed 116
mussels
    moules marinières 139
mustard seeds, pickled
    cucumbers with 86

N

nettle soup 121

O

onions and shallots 134-139
    see also spring (salad) onions
    balsamic roasted red onions
        138
    bean salad 38
    beetroot relish 45
    casserole of winter
        vegetables 195
    French onion soup 135
    gazpacho 202
    green tomato chutney 204
    homity pie 165
    Jansson's temptation 166
    Lancashire cheese and
        onion pie 137
    moules marinières 139
    pear and apple chutney 150
    piccalilli 64
    pissaladière 136
    pommes Lyonnaise 163
    roast chicory tart 75
    runner bean chutney 40
    shallot and tomato salad
        138
    young broad beans cooked
        with onion 36
oranges, salad of fennel and
    orange 94
oregano, balsamic roasted red
    onions 138
oriental sauce for asparagus 29

P

pancakes 220
pannacotta 216-217
Parma ham, with melon and
    strawberry salsa 190
Parmesan cheese
    cannelloni with peas and
        Gorgonzola 155
    celeriac and thyme gratin
        71
    chicory gratin 76
    leek pie (flamiche) 126
    Parmesan and thyme straws
        122
    pea and mint risotto 154
    roast chicken stuffed with
        courgettes under the skin 81
    roast pumpkin risotto 170
    rocket or basil pesto sauce
        114
parsley
    herb stuffing for fish 120
    homity pie 165
    parsley-stuffed Portobello
        mushrooms 116
    parsnip, carrot and bulgar
        wheat salad 141
    peas with prosciutto 153
    shallot and tomato salad 138
    tabbouleh 119
parsnips 140-144
    casserole of winter
        vegetables 195
    everyday roasted pumpkin
        or squash 168
    mashed parsnips and carrots
        143
    parsnip, carrot and bulgar
        wheat salad 141
    parsnip, chickpea and
        saffron soup 142
    parsnip crisps 143
    parsnips Molly Parkin 144
    sautéed parsnips 143
    warm winter vegetable salad
        141
pasta
    asparagus with cream and
        pasta 27
    broccoli with pasta 50
    cannelloni with peas and
        Gorgonzola 155
    cavolo nero sauce for penne
        68
    linguini with garlic and chilli
        98
    soupe Menerboise 78

tomato sauce for spaghetti 203

pastry *see also* pies, quiches, tarts
  filo with Chinese asparagus 29
  mille feuilles 211–2
  puff 210–211
  for quiches 209
  rich short crust 214
  sablée 214
  sweet crust 214

pavlova with raspberries 174

pears 145–150
  blue cheese salad dressing 132
  pear and apple chutney 150
  pear and blue cheese salad 146
  pears in red wine 149
  pears in sweetened white wine 149
  red cabbage with pears 56
  Springfield cake (pear and ginger sponge) 147–148
  tarte tatin 16

peas 151–155
  artichokes, peas and broad beans 21
  asparagus in a salad of pea shoots 26
  cannelloni with peas and Gorgonzola 155
  cold pea and mint soup 152
  everyday Indian cauliflower and potatoes 63
  lettuce and pea soup 131
  mangetouts, mixed beans with spices 35
  pea and lovage soup 152
  pea and mint risotto 154
  peas and beans with new potatoes 162
  peas with prosciutto 153
  purée of fresh peas 152
  sformato of peas 153
  steamed peas and lettuce 133

Pecorino cheese
  broad beans and Pecorino antipasti 34
  purple spouting broccoli with pickled walnuts and Pecorino cheese 49
  rocket or basil pesto sauce 114

peppers, green

gazpacho 202

peppers, red
  green tomato chutney 204
  Oriental spinach salad 187

pickles
  beetroot relish 45
  damson chutney 107
  pear and apple chutney 150
  pickled asparagus 30
  pickled beetroot 45
  pickled cucumbers with garlic and mustard seeds 86
  runner bean chutney 40
  sweet pickled greengages 160

pies *see also* tarts
  apple and blackberry pie 14
  homity pie 165
  Lancashire cheese and onion pie 137
  leek pie (flamiche) 126

pine nuts, cavolo nero sauce for penne 68
  rocket or basil pesto 114

pissaladière 136

plums and greengages 156–160
  crumble 181
  pie filling 14
  plum and almond tart 158
  plum clafoutis 159
  plum gratinée 157
  plum jam 157
  sweet pickled greengages 160

pomegranate seeds
  roasted cauliflower and hazelnut salad 62
  warm winter vegetable salad 141

porridge oats, cranachan 178

potatoes 161–166
  artichoke and potato soup 24
  baked new potatoes with sour cream and caviar 164
  broccoli and Stilton soup 48
  colcannon 66
  cumin potatoes 162
  everyday Indian cauliflower and potatoes 63
  everyday new potatoes 162
  everyday swedes 195
  homity pie 165
  Jansson's temptation 166
  nettle soup 121
  peas and beans with new potatoes 162

pommes Lyonnaise 163
  potato salad with a mayonnaise dressing 164
  potato salad with a vinaigrette dressing 164
  pumpkin with Raclette 169
  rösti with smoked salmon and watercress 165
  sweetcorn chowder 197
  Vichyssoise 124

prawns
  prawns and chives smörgås 114
  radicchio and prawn salad 73

prosciutto, peas with 153

pumpkins and squashes 167–170
  everyday roasted pumpkin or squash 168
  pumpkin and ginger soup 168
  pumpkin with Raclette 169
  roast pumpkin risotto 170
  roasted pumpkin seeds 169
  warm winter vegetable salad 141

Q

quiches *see also* tarts
  Swiss chard 199

quinces
  apple pie 14
  quince cheese 108

R

Raclette cheese, pumpkin with 169

radicchio *see* chicory, endive, radicchio and Treviso

radishes, salad of fennel, cucumber and radish 94

raisins
  green tomato chutney 204
  pear and apple chutney 150

raspberries 171–178
  blackcurrant coulis 88
  cranachan 178
  hot raspberry soufflés 173
  pavlova with raspberries 174
  raspberries and zabaglione 172
  raspberry and almond Eve's pudding 172
  raspberry coulis 175
  raspberry flummery 177

raspberry mousse 175
raspberry ripple ice cream 176
raspberry vinegar 178
summer pudding 106
unboiled raspberry jam 175
vanilla bean brulée with blackcurrants 90
rhubarb 179-184
cranachan 178
Mark Hix's Ricotta with spiced rhubarb 183
pie filling 14
rhubarb and grapefruit jam 183
rhubarb and orange cake 182
rhubarb cordial 184
rhubarb crumble 181
rhubarb ice cream 180
ribollita 67
rice pudding 215
Ricotta cheese
asparagus with cream and pasta 27
chopped spinach with Ricotta in puff pastry 211
Mark Hix's Ricotta with spiced rhubarb 183
Ricotta al forno with strawberries and marsala 193
roast chicken stuffed with courgettes under the skin 81
tomato roulade with Ricotta and basil 206
risottos
pea and mint 154
roast pumpkin 170
rocket
rocket or basil pesto sauce 114
rösti with smoked salmon and watercress 165
runner beans *see* beans, runner, French, Blue Lake and others

S
saffron
parsnip, chickpea and saffron soup 142
pears in sweetened white wine 149
salad dressings
anchovy and egg 133

blue cheese salad dressing 132
mayonnaise 212
Oriental dressing 187
vinaigrette 127
salads
asparagus in a salad of pea shoots 26
bean salad 38
carrot and cumin salad 59
carrot salad with chilli 59
cauliflower, radicchio and caper salad 74
cucumber salad 85
dandelion salad 118
Greek beetroot salad 43
leeks vinaigrette 127
lettuce salad 132
mango coleslaw 54
marrow salad 79
Oriental spinach salad 187
parsnip, carrot and bulgar wheat salad 141
pear and blue cheese salad 146
potato salad with a mayonnaise dressing 164
potato salad with a vinaigrette dressing 164
radicchio and prawn salad 74
raw artichoke salad 20
roasted cauliflower and hazelnut salad 62
salad of calabrese stalks 49
salad of fennel and orange 94
salad of fennel, cucumber and radish 94
shallot and tomato salad 138
sweetcorn and tomato salad 198
tabbouleh 119
tomato salad 202
warm winter vegetable salad 141
salmon, smoked, in rösti **165**
sauces
anchovy sauce 50
autumn fruit coulis 108
béchamel sauce 213
blackcurrant coulis 88
cavolo nero sauce for penne 68
cream sauce 50
gooseberry sauce for

mackerel 100
horseradish sauce 116
lemon butter sauce for asparagus 27
Marie Rose sauce 212
mint sauce 118
oriental sauce for asparagus 29
raspberry coulis 175
rémoulade 72
rocket or basil pesto sauce 114
strawberry salsa 190
shallots *see* onions and shallots
sloe gin 110
sorrel
sorrel butter 114
sorrel sauce for veal 100
sorrel soufflé 115
soufflés
courgette and goat's cheese soufflé 80
hot apple and Calvados soufflé 13
hot raspberry soufflés 173
hot strawberry soufflé 192
sorrel soufflé 115
soups
artichoke and potato soup 24
asparagus soup 28
borscht 42
broccoli and Stilton soup 48
chilled lettuce and celery soup 130
cold pea and mint soup 152
courgette soup 78
cream of celery soup 70
French onion soup 135
gazpacho 202
lettuce and pea soup 131
nettle soup 121
parsnip, chickpea and saffron soup 142
pea and lovage soup 152
pumpkin and ginger soup 168
ribollita 67
soupe Menerboise 78
sweetcorn chowder 197
tarator 84
Vichyssoise 124
spinach 185-188
Chinese spinach 186
chopped spinach with Ricotta in puff pastry 211

épinards en purée 186
everyday spinach 186
Oriental spinach salad 187
Penny's carrot and spinach
    terrine 58
soufflé 115
wilted spinach with
    cannellini beans and
    tomatoes 188
spring (salad) onions
    cod with fennel, leeks and
        tomatoes 95
    leek fritters with soured
        cream dressing 128
    Oriental spinach salad 187
    radicchio and prawn salad
        74
    tabbouleh 119
    tomato keftedes 205
squashes see pumpkins and
    squashes
Stilton cheese, broccoli and
    Stilton soup 48
strawberries 189-193
    hot strawberry soufflé 192
    melon and Parma ham with
        strawberry salsa 190
    old fashioned strawberry
        shortcake 191
    Ricotta al forno with
        strawberries and marsala
        193
swedes 194-195
    casserole of winter
        vegetables 195
    everyday swedes 195
sweet Cicely 113
sweet potatoes
    everyday roasted pumpkin
        or squash 168
    warm winter vegetable salad
        141
sweetcorn 196-198
    sweetcorn and tomato salad
        198
    sweetcorn cakes 198
    sweetcorn chowder 197
    sweetcorn with spiced butter
        197
Swiss chard 199-200
    alternative to spinach 185
    everyday Swiss chard 197
    quiche 196
    Swiss chard gratin 197

T
tabbouleh 119
tarts see also quiches
    asparagus and goat's cheese
        tarts 32
    leek tart (tarte aux poireaux)
        125
    pissaladière 136
    plum and almond tart 158
    redcurrant Mazarin tart 89
    roast chicory tart 75
    tarte aux pommes 17
    tarte Tatin 16
tayberries, summer pudding
    106
thyme
    celeriac and thyme gratin
        71
    chicken liver pâté with
        thyme 117
    Parmesan and thyme straws
        122
    parsnips Molly Parkin 144
    thyme-roasted beetroot 44
tomatoes 201-206
    borlotti ratatouille 39
    braised celery hearts 70
    broccoli with pasta 50
    cod with fennel, leeks and
        tomatoes 95
    courgette soup 78
    everyday Indian cauliflower
        and potatoes 63
    gazpacho 202
    green tomato chutney 204
    mixed beans with spices 35
    parsnip, carrot and bulgar
        wheat salad 141
    parsnips Molly Parkin 144
    pissaladière 136
    runner bean chutney 40
    shallot and tomato salad
        138
    sundried tomatoes in the
        oven 203
    sweetcorn and tomato salad
        198
    tabbouleh 119
    tomato keftedes 205
    tomato roulade with Ricotta
        and basil 206
    tomato salad 202
    tomato sauce for spaghetti
        203
    tomatoes à la Provençale
        202

wilted spinach with
    cannellini beans and
    tomatoes 188
Treviso see chicory, endive,
    radicchio and Treviso
turnips 207-208
    casserole of winter
        vegetables 195
    glazed turnips 208
    roast chicory tart 75
Vichyssoise 124

W
waffles 219
walnuts
    blue cheese salad dressing
        132
    purple spouting broccoli
        with pickled walnuts and
        Pecorino cheese 49
    spiced roasted walnuts 111
    walnut leaf liqueur 111
watercress
    courgette soup 78
    puréed in mayonnaise 212
    rösti with smoked salmon
        and watercress 165
whisky 178
wine, pears in red wine 149

Y
yoghurt, tarator 84

BIOGRAPHIES

Susan Williamson's cooking experience grew from her parents' hotel in
Cornwall to hosting foreign students and cooking for family and friends.
She worked as a picture researcher, spending 17 years at
Penguin Books before turning freelance.

Carrie Hill has illustrated many books and magazines, specialising in
textiles, crafts, decorative maps, food and cookery. This book has been a
joy to work on and she has enjoyed the tasty samples.
carriehill99@yahoo.co.uk   www.carriehill-art.com

Sally Geeve is a graphic designer who has worked extensively in
publishing; children's books, encyclopedias, corporate accounts... and now
this glorious book about her two favourite topics – gardening and cookery.
geeve@blueyonder.co.uk   www.sallygeeve.com

Rosemary Cole, who has prepared the index, and the author met
as undergraduates at UEA.

A second volume of recipes,
based around cooking with herbs,
is underway.